The Immigrant Writers Association, in producing these anthologies, does immense service to not only the authors of these stories but to readers all over the world.

I found the synchronicities and universal themes woven to be absolutely delightful.

~ Grant Leishman for Readers' Favorite

FINDING THE WAY

IMMIGRANT WRITERS ASSOCIATION

RACHEL LAWERH   MARÈME DIONGUE

NEIL GONSALVES   OLESYA KOLISNYK

RAMONA VIZITIU   PAUL LEBEDEV

MARNI DIEANU   KIMBERLY J. KIRT

GABRIELA CASINEANU   ALKA KUMAR

EMANUEL PETRESCU   BRIAN SANKARSINGH

YANNIS LOBAINA

IWA

Book Cover Design, Formatting: Gabriela Casineanu

Library and Archives Canada Cataloguing in Publication

IWA Immigrant Writers Association, 2022

ISBN Paperback: 978-1-7779081-2-6

ISBN Electronic book: 978-1-7779081-1-9

CONTENTS

WHERE I SET MY ANVIL

BY RACHEL LAWERH

All immigrants I meet in this country have a story of why they came here. It is usually with high hopes of something better.

A new beginning, a new chance, an opportunity to do differently. My own story was not different.

My grandmother had always said that the men who forged metal were the ones who used to be kingmakers. She would smack her lips and say it with pride, that her family forged metal, every single one of them … including her mother. She would talk about how the heat of the fire spoke to the body in ways that people will never know.

"If you forged metal …" she would say while staring blankly ahead, "… you knew rage and fury, you also knew reason, grace, and tact. It's the fire's gift to you; it injects it … furiously into your veins, through that hard red heat that takes you over every day." She would heave her shoulders up, slowly every time and hunch her back, then she would try to lift her now withered arms, perhaps to make the motion of a hammer striking the anvil, but her hands could not stay up long enough to finish. Her voice would seem distant as she continued, "And when the anvil fell, the whole community had to gather to carry it. It was too heavy to be borne by one, even one as powerful as the metal forger." I had questions; why was it falling in the first place if it was that heavy? She would look at me and shake her head; it was the kind of headshake you do towards loving children who had hurt themselves and were crying but still would not let go of their instrument of hurt because they were too young to understand that it was what was causing them pain. That kind of headshake.

"If you give a man all the power; if he rode the fire and metal, the leaders of the land and the anvil; what do you suppose will happen?" Her deep piercing eyes fell on me.

The first time I heard her ask, I did not think of what would happen quickly enough so she responded with a quiet tone, "He will no longer feel human, and he will destroy everything that is needed for his own survival."

You see, grandma at a certain point had an onset of dementia, and sometimes she did not remember who I was unless I laid my head on her lap and put her hands in my hair. The only time she spoke with some certainty was when she talked of the metal forgers so, from the first time she told me this story when I was a teenager, I made sure to ask again, feigning ignorance about the forged metal, the anvil, and the power each time I visited. So, she narrated the same story over and over again.

I remember clearly the day of her funeral. "Come away Yvie, you have sat with her for too long. There are other people waiting to say goodbye." My mother whispered this to me. But I could not take my eyes off my grandmother, clad in her white dress with lace gloves, and with a wig on her head. She would have objected to the ridiculous outfit. She would have wanted to be wrapped in a cloth, a richly patterned dumas wax print, one wrapped around her waist with an identical one on her chest with puff sleeves, then another sitting majestically on her head. That was how she had always presented herself. That was how she would have liked to join her people.

I soaked in the last image of her as my mother gently tugged me out of the tent. I heard a wail from one of the women who hurriedly brushed past me into the tent as I went out.

That was the last memory I had of Afiyo lying in state. Her obituary had read '*beloved, fruitful and home maker*'. Fruitful? Because she had raised ten children and had twelve grandchildren and six great-grandchildren? Or was it because all her children and descendants were doing well? It could not have been, of course; there was me. The little dent in the corner. Struggling when all others had figured out where they wanted to be. *Who comes from a line of metal forgers and kingmakers and still struggles?*

Afiyo herself, at age twenty-four, had left her father's home and married a man, one who was strong enough, befitting their family. It was said that, when Afiyo brought this man home, her father made him stand in the iron shed, blowing the fire and striking the iron when it was pulled out hot. It was a test to see if he was strong enough to be with the most challenging daughter. He passed, and they had two sets of twins, then the next set of twins and the rest of their children. It was said that their home was so fruitful that women who wanted children rubbed on their gates while they said a prayer for Afiyo's luck. Afiyo and her husband started what would become the biggest daycare in their community. Afiyo leveraged their already large family; people trusted that their children were safe with them, and soon, they had a whole lot of women dropping off and picking up their children for a fee. Then they added teachers, added more land, and voila! The first community school at the exact time education was becoming a huge event in their predominantly farming community. Even though the line of forging metal had ended with her mother, Afiyo started and founded something for herself. So did her children and their grandchildren. Afiyo's children were the ones who had first left the village to make it to the schools in the big cities. It was her grandchildren who drew people to watch them on the television debates. It was her children who built the biggest house in the town and tarred the road. Even the great-grandchildren at their ages were known for something. Then there was me, Afiyo's clear favourite but the only person who did not have anything going on. Every year, I watched my parents say something about my twin, how he had many offers coming in and how he was unable to choose where to be because they were all too good. He could not join the family reunions, but he contributed greatly financially. I listened quietly as my uncles and aunties spoke about their children, what they did and how well it was going for them. Everyone was careful not to ask anything of me even though I was right there. It was as if there had been a hushed discussion in my absence, a mutual agreement that I would be left out of any discussion regarding success. My cousins were particularly polite, everyone would chat about what they did but conveniently skipped me, just as the job and marriage market were skipping me. It was always as if I was a shadow, present, but not present. It did not help that conversations and jokes revolved around work; "Oh, my co-worker did this! This happened at a work party … I met this guy at a work event." I had less and less to contribute, so I took to sitting at the edge of the table, unseen and unheard, yet not showing up in December was never a thought in my mind. So, every year, I went … until one year my parents asked, as I spoke about the reunion, whether I would really like to go. It was strange, considering I always went with them. I had always enjoyed those near-quiet long drives with them, full of music I heard only during my childhood.

It had puzzled me; it took me more time than it should have to arrive at the conclusion that perhaps they did not want me to go. I wished I had made it all up in my head, that my mother would respond, "Nonsense thought is that!" in that sweet young tone of hers, but "That is good Yvie, it did not look like you enjoy events, you could spend the time doing something productive" was the response that showed how they really felt. Even my father had looked away, pretending to be scouting something on the ceiling. It was Christmas, and there was nothing more productive than being with family, but I accepted, adding that I had a couple of friends' events to attend. And that was one of the things I disliked about myself —erasing myself so everyone but me felt good. I could have asked them why, I could have said that I needed to see my grandmother, whose company I enjoyed … but I said nothing, just like those other times when my young self came home with my report card, and I was sad that I was first in the class because my brother would not be first, and I would hear my father berate him, "Do you see how your sister keeps taking the first position every time? Why are you not like her?" It did not improve when I skipped a class ahead of him; "You have sat down for your sister to move beyond you …" so I took to downplaying my awards. "I think they let me on the debate team because Madam Betty liked me. I think I made school prefect because none of the others will do it." All so my brother did not have to feel bad, and my father would have nothing to compare. It had changed nothing that I down-played my achievements; my brother did not become my friend, but I could not stop. If someone said my clothes were nice, I quickly responded, "It is really an old item, your clothes are way nicer." If someone said, "That is a brilliant point you are making," I would spend time focusing on another person's point, explaining why it was better. It was no surprise to me that I missed the opportunity to speak about the elephant that had been in the room ever since I finished my master's degree and had no job. Once again, the ever-docile obedient child who got nothing but a few pats on the back in the present and a lifetime of shame for taking decisions that others made for her.

In fact I met him that Christmas. It had been unbearable and awfully quiet in my parents' house … knowing everyone was out there living without me made me want to have a celebration of my own, a celebration of my nothingness. *When was the last time you went anywhere with yourself or with a man?* I was young and beautiful, and that I had not succeeded in the job market did not mean I could not succeed in the other departments of life. So I decided to connect with the man from my university class who had been my friend through the program. It had been clear he liked me a lot more than as a friend. The date had been somewhat stale, it lacked a spark, that "he is the one!" feeling that everyone spoke about.

But that was another one of my problems, wanting to follow all the rules and applying them in the order that people said they should be. *Was that not what had gotten me here?* In school, I was brilliant. I solved problems the way I was taught to. I navigated life the way my parents had taught me to, but how was that working out? Maybe the old script of life was dead —it was up to me to write a new script. So I married the man without the spark. Everyone had seemed happy—my first win on the family adult table of life. He was a doctor, a charming doctor. At the family gatherings, he spoke for me; I did not need to speak. Everyone was eager to hear what he had to say. You see, my family had teachers, lawyers, businessmen, and pilots, but not a doctor. His experiences were a new addition, and everyone had a neck pain or a sudden occasional headache that they would want to hear his opinion on. Even though I was still a shadow at the table, I had a representative. He went from being *Yvie's husband* to *Doc* and then to *Kofi;* sometimes, it went as far as *son.* I watched my parents trade me up for another successful son while I withered away in the background. Nobody saw that my weight had kept falling. I did not have large bones like the other members of my house, but I had moderate assets that unmistakably stood out; now they too faded in the shadows. Nobody saw that his grips on my arm were tighter, or that he sent me on errands around the table. "Yvie honey, get me a glass of water; Yvie, could you bring out the plaque in the car; Yvie, bring out the gifts …" as he told one story or the other about an award he won, a dinner he had with a minister, or a complicated surgery he had done. He was their son now, and I was the stranger. Everyone crowded around him, and no one noticed that my lips had slightly protruded to the left. Or that my sunglasses grew bigger at each function to cover much of my face, or that my makeup got heavier and thicker. Not even my parents noticed that I visited them less and less even when I lived just an hour away from them. No one noticed that his hands on my back were to keep me in line and had nothing to do with affection.

No one but Afiyo, and she had resorted to telling me vigorously the stories of the metal forging women and men. Those she had met, and those she heard of through her mother. At every visit, as she sat proudly in her armchair that rocked back and forth, she would pat my hair and I would cry, never saying a word about my sorrow, but she knew, just as she had always known. She would tell me the story again, grinding her teeth in anger.

"You knew rage and fury, you also knew reason, grace, and tact. It's the fire's gift to you; it injects it … furiously into your veins, through that hard red heat that takes you over every day."

Her hands would stroke my hair firmly but gently as she hissed. Sometimes her voice reduced to a growl when she uttered the words I had come to know so well. Sometimes her hands discovered new additions on my body, a scar on my arm that had not been there the visit before, a bloody bump on my head, a red patch of swollen skin on my neck, carefully nested under my hair.

"If you give a man all the power; if he rode the fire and metal, and he rode the leaders of the land and the anvil; what do you suppose will happen?" She would growl the rest of her story.

She had been the only member of my family who had not been completely taken by my husband. Everyone who joined my family by birth or marriage was introduced to the matriarch. She would be escorted to the hall, and proper greetings would be said. Before my marriage, when Kofi was first introduced, she never asked him "Ibi, k3 o ng3 k33?" *(How are you, my son?)*. She merely nodded at him, never acknowledging him with the traditional "my son". It was puzzling, but everyone believed Afiyo was growing old and was maybe forgetting culture. But over the years, even Kofi himself came to understand that he could trick everyone in the family apart from Afiyo.

And as the dementia grew worse, all I needed to do was place my head on her lap and her hands in my hair—that was all it took for the story to begin. It had gaps and long pauses, but she told it anyway.

. . .

Her funeral had been the day of my awakening. I had longed to hear her struggle to say *"He will no longer feel human, and he will destroy everything that is needed for his own survival."* I longed to hear the grinding of her teeth as she said those words. The only line of the story that she remembered as time went by. It had always given me some strength—a false feeling of power —that I would walk out of her dark room to the outside and tell the family to help me lift the anvil. But once I stepped out, he was right outside the door, waiting to grip my hands firmly and lead me home to the never-ending reign of terror.

His hands had slid into mine that day, that familiar squeeze that said "trouble", and my mind shifted to think about my grandmother's *'beloved, fruitful and homemaker'* obituary. No one had thought to include that she was a powerful woman who was the family head, in a culture where men were the head by birth. No one had thought to include that she rallied the men of her family for a 10-year battle with encroaching miners that saw her winning the community's land back. Neither did they mention that none of her late husband's family dared more than whisper regarding the properties they owned together. They had known they would never be able to win a fight against the one who fought off a corporation, so they peddled rumours that she had a hand in his death. She had stood unshaken and unfazed during the funeral as they sang spiteful songs in metaphors. In fact, she herself was said to have sung one in response, and their tongues were bridled instantly.

She had known and understood me even when I was a child. Every time she stroked my hair and told me stories of the metal forgers, she was trying to remind me of the power I possess within me, that I was powerful too and could make changes, demand what I desired, and ask for help. I longed for her to stroke my hair one more time … I needed that false sense of power I always felt after her story. And as my husband led me out to the car park, I realized that I had lost my only source of comfort. The realization felt deeper with each step as Kofi tugged on my hand towards the car. Everyone was staying until well after the funeral, but Kofi wanted to leave on the day of her burial. She was still lying in state, but he would not let me watch them lower my beloved grandmother into the ground. He would not let me throw my favourite jewel in her grave with her casket. He was cutting all my connection with her even in the afterlife. I froze and could not move, and I looked helplessly at my feet; *this was indeed going to be the rest of my life.*

"Let's go! What are you doing? I will be late!" He had pulled on my arm. Dropping his charming husband persona as he raised his voice, that low growl creeping in. "Yvie! I do not like this thing you are about to start; you will regret it. What has come over you? Is this how a married woman behaves? We discussed how long we will be here, I have things to do and here you are, acting like a child with no work or ambitions! You better move your legs or … !" His voice was raised.

"Or what?!" a deeper voice asked him. I did not need to look up to see who it was … I knew as tears fell down my face.

"Or what will you do Kofi?! This is her grandmother's funeral! This is a family event that she wants to be present for, you can either support her through it or you can find your way out."

My eyes never left my feet, and my feet never moved and neither did my brother's hand on my shoulder, not even as the rain poured down, blessing grandmother's memory and perhaps my first act of defiance.

· · ·

"Why did you not tell mummy?" My brother asked, "Why did you not say something?" I had considered not responding … *was it not time for me to let others not be at peace as well?*

So, I spoke out. It became more than Afiyo's burial; it was also a reconciliation and a time to heal. It became a time of freedom; my marriage to the man whose second career was kickboxing at home was over. He had my things wrapped up and ready when I returned to my matrimonial home … in the company of my brother, my parents, my cousins, my aunties, and the nephews and nieces. The reunion was at his house. Everyone had a word to say to him. I could not cry; I was so awash with emotion that I could only laugh.

I could hear Afiyo's voice saying, "And when the anvil fell, the whole community had to gather to carry it. It was too heavy to be borne by one, even one as powerful as the metal forger."

My community had gathered to lift my anvil.

And they gathered again when I found my purpose … there I was, that day at the airport laughing and receiving a list of things they would like me to give them when I returned. There I was at what they would call the prime of my life, a nearly middle-aged woman, with a failed marriage record and no child, on a plane to begin life in a country where I knew no one. I wondered what my family had thought. Maybe they were happy for me. Maybe for once, they understood that I was making a decision for myself, one that only I made. I was following the principles that only I believed. Maybe the real reason I had followed the scripted path of life was that I was too afraid of responsibility and accountability. It is easier to say, "I followed the path my parents dictated to me, and today, I have no child, no decent job, and or money of my own." It was a safety net to cushion against hard choices. It is a story to which a lot of people will be sympathetic. As compared to saying; "I deviated from what my parents and society asked me to do, and here I am, suffering and unsuccessful." But I had come to realize that was a much more powerful story. All who made their path dealt with it. There was always a risk it would never work out, *but what if it did?*

That what-if was why I got on the plane to seek more education when the first two degrees I had earned had never been used. But I had other motives—for me, this move meant a different life, a new life, someplace where I could be whoever I desired. I had thirsted for this place where I could suddenly reverse who I was. I could become the extrovert, the one who asked the most questions, the one who did not shy away from confrontation. A place where I could say "This is who I am" without anyone saying, "Are you not the woman from three years ago with no self-worth and no success story, the one whose marriage was broken and who could not speak up?"

I dreamt this new life would be different, and it was.

The air was different, the people were different, and the land was different.

Everything was different in a way that was unexpected. Like at the airport when my seat number was changed, and I was moved farther back perhaps to make room for someone more deserving. Or when I read of an opportunity and scrolled quickly to the bottom to find out if it could apply to me as well or was for only the people of the land. Or when I woke up in a panic at night, wondering what my next steps should be so I too can forge a path of success. Or when I spoke eloquently, and people complimented my knowledge. Everyone here who looked like me seemed the same; they all seemed to be forging something; the people on the bus, in their cars, at the store, on the street … every one of them, I like to think.

· · ·

The land here, despite being welcoming and full of opportunities, had a way of reminding me that I am not its chosen one. But I have never been the chosen one anywhere, not even in the land where my ancestors lived and breathed. But this is the place I chose to forge my own metal; this is where I set my anvil.

ABOUT THE AUTHOR

Rachel Lawerh

Rachel Lawerh is a Public Health Professional, Photographer, and Creative Writer.

She is a PhD student (Population Health) at the University of Ottawa, where she focuses on how our social, political, and economic environment influences our behaviour and health.

Her creative storytelling highlights social justice issues documented through the lived experiences of Ghanaians as they navigate various aspects of their lives.

As a firm believer in the economic empowerment of girls and women, she founded MoonValley Foundation, an organization dedicated to the economic empowerment of girls through vocational training.

Connect with Rachel Lawerh:

- Rachellawerh.com
- Linkedin.com/in/rachel-l-

THE DISASTER

BY MARÈME DIONGUE

Imagine a ticking bomb. Now, imagine you found that bomb and warned everyone around the perimeters about it. They'd run away, right? Or maybe try to find a way to disarm the bomb. They might even try to move the bomb for the detonation to occur elsewhere, in a safe area. Well, imagine they just did nothing. Imagine all the people you warned just … sat and watched as the ticking continued, slowly but surely bringing you all closer to death.

Tic … tic … tic… tic … tic … tic …

One hour away from death would turn into two minutes and so on until the final three seconds. And then... BOOM, everyone would die. Sounds inconceivable, right? Dystopian? A horror movie maybe? Well, that is the exact hell I lived, and this is the story.

I was just finishing my post-doctoral research. A young marine biologist, I was passionate about oceanography and the mysteries the sea had yet to reveal. And oh boy! Did the sea have a surprise for us! During my research in the north at the

Australian Center for Oceanic Research, my team and I discovered an anomaly. Something we'd never seen before. Something that could, no, that WOULD kill us all. I foolishly believed that this fact alone would be enough to shake the world into action. The world's response? They shut us down and swept everything under the rug. I thought I was going insane. How could we be the only ones panicking? There was something down there, far more dangerous than any asteroid, far more newsworthy than any celebrity scandal, far more urgent than all the wars combined, yet the government and media stood idly by.

"What can we do?" Milly, our team's navigator, asked. "If none of the officials in power care, how can we get the message out there?"

"Get the message out there?! You must be out of your mind! The government shut us up because there should be no message! We're all gonna die! Might as well let people live peacefully!" Gert, our data analysis researcher, replied with emotion.

"How could you say such a thing, Gert! They all deserve to know! You want to keep a fucking sea creature capable of destroying the world as we know it hidden from the people? We could put a stop to this."

"Stop it?!! Are you—"

Clide, our team leader, decided to intervene at this point.

"There is no use in fighting. The truth is that making such a decision is not up to us. As scientists, we have a moral and ethical obligation to share our knowledge with the world, and as humans, we were to protect our planet."

It was as simple as that.

"Let the politicians take care of the people's reaction, let them soothe the people's minds and lead them; our only job is to inform."

If the influential people wouldn't broadcast our message, we'd have to do it ourselves. We set out to film a documentary using Anya's cinematographic equipment and our remaining budget. Every detail of our discovery would be shared. From the creature's discovery to the significance of its arrival. After we had synthesized our information, we needed to find a way to distribute it and spread the word. We had to be quick and create a buzz before our voices were silenced. We knew social media would be both our best and worst option. It has the potential to reach thousands in a second, but we could be banned just as quickly, and once discovered, there was no turning back. We decided to gamble for it either way, and it worked. With a bit of hacking, we managed to broadcast our documentary on thousands of platforms.

In less than an hour, millions of people had watched, shared, reposted, and commented on our documentary. Many believed it was a joke or a divine call. Some people created memes; others made tweets. We didn't care. Our job was done. The message had been delivered. I held on to the belief that after the first wave of astonishment, people would come to their senses and do something about it. But a month later, no one talked about it anymore. The buzz had not compelled politicians to act, people had dismissed it as a false alarm, the scientific world had remained silent, and the media had not taken the matter seriously. The rest of the world seemed unconcerned. Gert had dropped out of the project and isolated himself in a remote area. Milly had gone mad and committed the unthinkable. Clide had gone back to his home-land Canada. Anya had become a renowned cinematographer thanks to the documentary, and the rest of the team had been dissolved. Moon and I were the only ones to have stayed.

Why? Because we had nowhere to go, because the research wasn't done, because we wanted to die trying. We stayed, with no budget and no workspace, just us and the equipment that was left.

"No way!!! That's so cool!" *yelled Kane.*

"Shut up Kane! Let her finish the story!" *pleaded Lance.*

Khadi burst out laughing. She went on …

We worked near the waters of the Coral Sea in the Australian northeast, not too far from what was once known as Brisbane. The site used to be lovely but by then, corals were already dying, and ecosystems were collapsing. What we were interested in wasn't the coral reefs, but the Kramid Orchae, a sea creature we had recently discovered. A new species, never seen before. We'd found only one specimen at the time. It looked like a waspfish with the head of a chameleon. The creature wasn't big, six to seven inches long and two to three inches wide. Its anatomy was most impressive, it had incredible defence mechanisms, and it could survive months with no food and weeks with no water. We estimated the individual could live up to two hundred years. I can't express how surprised I was to see no reaction from the scientific community to this discovery. Nobody else seemed to be interested. It almost felt as if they knew something we didn't know, as if we had just discovered a new rock or something insignificant …. Our research led us to discover that the Kramid Orchae came from the deep sea, pretty far from the lands actually in the Pacific Ocean, the unexplored part of the oceans to which mankind had no access.

"THE DEEP SEA?!?!" *This time it was Adria.*

"Oh for God's sake! SHUT UP!" *yelled Lance with a glare.*

All right, calm down now! As I was saying ... the creature did not belong anywhere near the surface of the earth. Humans should not have known of such a species for at least another century until we'd explored the oceans a bit more. So what was it doing there? Why did we come across it? We spent months trying to figure out what was going on and how likely it was that this could happen, but nothing came of it. Being out of ideas and resources, Moon and I decided to contact Clide. He'd been our leader and had the most experience in marine biology and deep-sea exploration. Clide had dissolved the team after Milly's passing. They had been extremely close and honestly, the entire team was expecting the two to get married. Clide had gone back to his home city, Toronto, and had begun a new life. He would not reply to calls, emails, or text messages. He did not use social media or work on any science related projects; he'd completely abandoned his past life. Moon and I had agreed not to insist on bringing him back to the project that had caused him so much pain, but we needed him this once. We paid for our tickets to Canada with the little savings we had and set ourselves on a road to find him and bring him back.

"CANADA??? Where is that?" *inquired Gladys.*

"It doesn't exist anymore, you Doofus!" *Lance retorted sarcastically.*

"It was up in the north, it shared a border with America, remember? Gladys, I showed you on an old map?" *Fodé replied calmly.*

"OHHHHHHH, okay then, keep going Khadi!"

Laughter erupted.

Khadi continued ...

Where was I ... ah yes, Toronto, a beautiful city indeed, I wish you'd seen the world when it was all buildings and people. Clide was quite hard to find. We only had his full name, a rough idea of his appearance, and the city he lived in. To be honest, we had absolutely no plan going into this! Moon and I booked a hotel room and decided we'd try a bit of research. Clide had appeared in the documentary that millions of people had watched, someone on the internet must have recognized him and posted it! Our guess had been right. Clide had been spotted in different areas around a district named Scarborough, and we even discovered a small online community that, believing in our documentary, had started initiatives to help the cause.

"Wait ... wait ... wait ... you keep talking about this DANGER and a CAUSE, but what exactly can a tiny lizard-looking creature do to the planet?" *interrupted a perplexed Bailey.*

Ah, I omitted that part, didn't I?

This tiny creature, you see, had always lived deep, deep, deep in the sea. The environment down there influenced what it ate and its size. Because of the extreme pressure in the deep sea, Kramid Orchae would only be five to seven inches long and two to three inches wide, but up in the surface they could grow kilometres! It's also worth noting that whatever they ate down there was not available here, so their nutritional habits changed quickly, and the Kramid began feeding on land. Yes, literal land ... sand, soil ... the material that makes up our planet's crust. This explains why we discovered it near the Coral Sea. The creature we had found was feeding on the dead coral reef and nearby land. Worst of all, and most intriguingly, Kramid Orchae seemed to produce H_2O, aka water, after feeding. This creature would consume earthly products and produce water in the same way that plants produce oxygen through photosynthesis. Water that is completely normal and drinkable!

"Ewwww ... does that mean you tasted it?" *questioned Tamil.*

"I give up ... they just won't keep their mouths shut."

"Lance!" *said Khadi with a joyful but reproachful look.*

She went on ...

And yes, Tamil, I eventually tasted the produced water ... actually you all have!

"WHAT??" *exclaimed the children collectively.*

Ah now! Don't panic!

She chuckled.

Allow me to finish. The danger wasn't necessarily the Kramid Orchae itself but its migration to the surface. We had only encountered one specimen, but we had spotted a few more unknown sea creatures, and we had a bad feeling more were coming. That's where Clide's expertise comes in. Turns out that back in Toronto he couldn't help but work on this project and had secretly continued his research! He reasoned that the sudden appearance of this species was due to climate change as the waters had warmed up, and warmer surface water can't mix as well with the much colder deep sea water. The issue is that the level of oxygen in deep sea water depends on the warmer surface water. They must mix in order for the deep sea to receive enough oxygen. The deep sea's oxygen levels were already low, but with climate change, it had become a major issue. Sea creatures were migrating to higher sea levels, and populations would eventually mix. Kramid Orchaes were our first case, but we had no idea what else might come to the surface.

When the team was still together, we had known only about the Kramid Orchae's fascinating water-producing abilities. That alone had been enough to alarm us because the addition of water to our sea levels in big enough quantities could engulf our lands and drown our cities. After Clide, Moon, and I did added research, the level of urgency had become even greater. If Kramid Orchae populations migrated to the surface, they would devour our land, engulf the remainder of our lands with water and grow immensely due to the lack of pressure on their bodies. We'd also have to deal with other creatures finding themselves at sea levels different from their original ones. We were bewildered. What could we do? With this new information, we tried to contact the old team or at least what remained of it. Gert had gone MIA, and there was no way he'd be found. We reached out to Anya, the newly famous cinematographer. To our surprise she had spurned us, labelling us crazy. Anya promised to refute anything we'd say and even claim that Kramid Orchaes were nothing but fake news.

"WHAT A B--CH!" *yelled a random kid.*

Hey! Language! Anyway ... back to what I was saying ... Clide, Moon, and I were all on our own. The world had already turned its back on the issue; there was no second chance.

"So you gave up??" *asked a confused Kane.*

"I'm seriously going to choke you!" *exclaimed Lance.*

"Ok, ok, we get it Lance! Go on Khadi ..."

Thank you! Well we couldn't give up. But we focused on the only people who would believe us!

"THE ONLINE COMMUNITY" *said a kid in the back.*

Yes! Precisely! We reached out to them and started project Kramid 509.

"What a boring name!" *Lance blurted this out.*

Everyone's gaze was drawn to Lance.

"WHAT? You've all been commenting! Why not me then? Keep going Khadi!" *The boy had turned red.*

Khadi inhaled deeply ...

Well, it might not be the most beautiful name but that was the least of our concerns at the time. The community was pretty diverse, we came from all parts of the world and had varied knowledge and experiences. The goal of Project 509? Save humanity and keep records.

Now we weren't idealists, we knew we could not save the billions of people on Earth and its biodiversity but if we could just save even a small percentage, people who could tell the story, then we would have succeeded. We started building four bunkers thanks to the help of Jaftar Elhemoudi, a billionaire who'd joined our community, and Krawson Yanders, a landowner. We agreed the project would be kept secret, the world wasn't paying much attention to us anyway, and it was a good precaution that we decided we'd fool governments into thinking we'd gone mad about our research. And so over the span of a decade, we built four top secret bunkers. Each bunker was equipped to be inhabited by about a thousand citizens and withstand extreme pressures and amounts of water.

"WHOA, so you built our home?" *said an admiring Kane.*

"So our Bunks is not the only one? There are three more out there?" *questioned Seb.*

Yes, well actually four.

"What?? But you said you built four bunkers? Minus ours, that makes three, right?" *replied a four-year-old.*

Wow, Milly! Your counting skills have improved! Well, it's because we officially built four bunkers, but Clide, Moon, and I decided to build a fifth one using our own resources.

"Why?!?" *Lance argued.*

Because it was all too suspicious for us. Why was the world so silent? This was a bible worthy story. Something any scientist would want to research. We couldn't have been the first to notice or be interested in this phenomenon. Something was off. The creation of the bunkers as well as the online community support were ... well, too easy and convenient. What were the odds that a billionaire and a major landowner would be part of that small online community and cover all of our needs and expenses with such ease? Clide believed that the world's governments were already aware of the phenomenon and that the public had been purposefully kept in the dark, allowing the leaders of the world and the rich to survive.

"NO WAY!!" *exclaimed the children.*

Yes way! And he was right. When all four bunkers were completed and the situation had become critical, world politicians and wealthy people suddenly started to vanish. The world got into a frenzy, and crime rates, food insecurity, and deaths increased. People were confused. Those living near bodies of water were the first to die. As more Kramid Orchae rose to the surface, they scared the people away. Suicide rates went up, people had to be sacrificed, and every day the population found itself a little more cramped up. There was dwindling living space, food, and leaders. Chaos. The world leaders had abandoned their people and retreated to their bunkers. The truth had come to light.

They knew this was going to happen, governments around the world had formed alliances, agreeing to abandon their people if it meant some of them could survive. Scientists around the world had been warned, silenced, and barred from participating. Those who had tried to inform the people had been discarded as "clout chasers", liars or fanatics. People started to put two and two together: research in specific areas had been restricted to prevent curious scientists from making these discoveries, the media had been ordered and bribed into covering everything up. Influencers were offered bunker spots in exchange for silence. Anyone who'd been aware of this plan and was against it had been murdered or otherwise silenced. We had also been part of this plan, all along. We'd been chosen by the government to investigate this phenomenon. Unbeknownst to us, they'd led us to this discovery and assisted us in the hope that we'd find a solution that could save them. They'd chosen our team because of our leader, Clide, a renowned scientist in the field who'd made significant contributions to the scientific world prior to an incident that no one was to talk about.

They had expected Clide and his team to make sense of all this and come up with a solution they'd be able to make use of later. It was all a ruse. Play wisely rather than forcefully. A magnificent masquerade. Everything had been meticulously planned. Anya had been part of the government team; she had leaked our documentary to the government officials, installed cameras in our quarters. She'd made certain that the rest of the world saw us as a farce. She'd been their informant.

When The Disaster, as we like to call it, came to happen, Clide, Moon, the construction workers, and I ... had been excluded from the four bunkers. Luckily the Bunks, our secret 5th bunker, was waiting for us! But it had been submerged before the other bunkers, and our team had to struggle to reach it and open it.

"But how did we end up here? This was a secret bunker for your team. Despite that fact, we number in the thousands?"

Liu inquired.

Well ... Moon, Clide, the rest of the team, and I felt uneasy about leaving so many to die when there was a lot of space remaining in the Bunks. We decided to leave a signal to help people find us and kept the Bunks open for five days. Although the entrance to the Bunks had to be sealed for us to be completely safe, we determined that we could open the valve for five days before the Bunks suffered significant damage. Many joined us, and after the five days had passed, we locked ourselves in for good. Moon and I eventually married, Clide adopted Lily and Ferg, and the other adults with us also had kids of their own!

"WOW!" A deep voice arose from the crowd of children. The man stood up and laughed. He approached Khadi and embraced her.

"It seems Khadi couldn't help but tell you the whole story! I hope she hasn't traumatized all you kids!"

Laughter ensued ... Moon continued:

"We had quite the journey fifteen years ago! But it was all worthwhile."

"What happens next, Khadi? We can't stay here forever, can we?" *one of the children inquired.*

As Khadi sat in front of this new generation, reflecting on the new world they had to survive in, her late father's old adage came to mind: "In life, you must keep going, remember your roots, but keep soaring to the sky like a tree. When you are lost, return to your roots; they will lead you in the right direction."

She turned around and said:

"We find our way back."

A chapter dedicated to my late father, who gave me the love of writing.

ABOUT THE AUTHOR

Marème Diongue

Previous contributor to an IWA anthology

Marème Racine Diongue is a second-generation immigrant; both her parents are Senegalese. She grew up in Toronto and is now in her senior year of high school.

Marème has always been highly engaged in her community and is currently Student Trustee on her school's Board.

She won a poetry award in 2019 and has contributed to two IWA anthologies, *Building Bridges* and *Grow Together*.

Marème is a reading and debating enthusiast.

FINDING MY WAY THROUGH THE COMPLEXITY OF CHAOS

BY NEIL GONSALVES

We walked out of Africa as one and circumnavigated this planet. From one we became many who prospered and multiplied through mutual cooperation and community. We knew little but adapted constantly; survival depended upon it. Life started out simple, but complexity increased, and social networks became more convoluted. Power and position developed, class and caste emerged, and some arbitrary lines on a map created countrymen and foes. Through millennia the social hierarchy became entrenched and social identity sedimented; the rules we live by evolved, but change on that front is always slow and painstaking. The catalyst for change is often harsh, including a great deal of suffering as perspectives clash and humanity demands recognition. Through it all, people have always sought a path to self-actualization, a journey to find themselves and their place in this complex world. If there is one constant in this existence, it is the human quest to always find the way forward.

My journey began more than four decades ago. A life is characterized by migration, where home has often been a state of mind rather than a physical location. Whether prompted by family or embarked upon individually, our migratory ways were driven by a constant quest to find a way forward, a place to call home where roots might take and permanence may not be illusory. In a twenty-first century society, that might seem like an archaic mental disposition given the ease with which people flow and settle around the planet. We live in an interconnected global village, yet the human desire for a place to call home remains a critical component of our sense of self. I have spent a lifetime searching for an identity and trying to find a space among the chaos we call life. I have travelled from the Indian subcontinent to the Middle East and onwards to Canada in search of home, in search of peace and a sense of belonging. Along the way I have invented and reinvented myself many times over, each time wondering if I had discovered my authentic self, being restless and uneasy and never sure whether the current phase was a rest stop on the journey or the destination I had been seeking. I cannot help but ponder whether that is even something that needs to be puzzled out; perhaps life is a constant march with no final destination. Perhaps the seeking of a destination is the very thing that prevents living in the present and accepting the unknown. I have heard it said that life is like driving in the dark; we cannot see beyond the illumination of our headlights, but as long as we keep moving forward, the once unseen path that lies ahead becomes constantly illuminated by our own forward momentum. We may only see a little bit of the road ahead at a time; perhaps that is all we need to find the way.

By the time I was born, my parents had already left their childhood home in India in search of a better life in the newly developing Middle East. Their country of choice was the United Arab Emirates and the city was Dubai, a place in its infancy which held great promise for a better tomorrow. There was a large contingent of expatriates from the Indian subcontinent there, and they would forge a new identity as

Non-Resident Indians living on an employment visa, providing the labour to build up this emerging economy. Make no mistake however; this was not home, this was a transitory port, one that welcomed visitors who would contribute to the objective of building a shining city in the desert. Productive capacity was the benchmark of inclusion, all were welcome if they had something to offer. The trade-off was a tax-free haven where one could build a nest egg insofar as that nest was eventually built somewhere else. It never felt like home. I distinctly recall conversations, interviews, and documentaries that highlighted how the local population viewed expatriates as temporary residents, expendable if the day ever came that their productive capacity diminished. The locals were explicit, this was not home, we were visitors in Arabia, and most of what we saw was a mirage in the sand. It is easy to lose sight of that fact. Everywhere I looked I saw people who looked like me and sounded like me, fellow travelers somewhere on their own journey. I held an Indian passport, even though I never lived there. In Dubai, my country of origin was considered to be India, and in India I was deemed a N.R.I. (Non-resident Indian), a distinction that marked us as one of those who had left. People with no real home and no sense of belonging.

I'm sure some of my thoughts and ideas about my childhood in Dubai are coloured by my past youthful naivety, but perception is so often reality. My accounts here may sound foreign to other travelers on a similar journey. I imagine they may even seem foreign to members of my own family who were arguably on the same journey with me; nonetheless the frames of reference we construct to understand and bring meaning to our lives are deeply personal. I am not immune to such distortions in thinking; I intellectually understand that fact. However I accept that forty-plus years on, my perceptions are all I have left when interpreting my past and contextualizing my present. From my perspective, Dubai was a strange place;

we called it home, and back then I probably would have thought about it that way. Looking back, it feels like a disconnected period in my life, one that I know I lived through but feel no connection to in any way. Memories are a funny thing. I know they shape and change to conform to the narrative I have probably replayed in my mind a million times over, but they are probably inaccurate or at least coloured by my present lens. Yet it is the only reality I know, the one I draw upon and the reference point I use when comprehending my past. The lasting ideas I came away with included the notion that we were third-tiered residents there, not citizens, never citizens. Back then, citizenship was not an option. I was an Indian who never lived in India and a local who was never a local in Dubai. Life taught me that the small local Arab population had to be preserved; its continuation depended on birthright and privilege, an understandable predicament given that we were living in their home and on their lands and outnumbered them significantly. The second tier I understood to be people from Britain who were also expatriates in Dubai. We never really referred to them as 'white,' a common term used here in Canada that would have been an accurate description. In retrospect I do not doubt that this population was also diverse and multi-faceted, but it is not how I viewed it then. I saw them as the people who lived in villas on the beach and whose children went to prestigious private schools with class trips to Switzerland, while we went to the local parks or the hot springs out in the desert.

We were in the last tier, a complex grouping with a wide demographic range that included an entire spectrum from the wealthy business families to the labour class. My family was situated somewhere near the lower half of the middle of that range. We lived comfortably; my life was hardly what one would consider difficult. I remember my father working all day and running several businesses at night; my mother stayed home and raised us until we were approximately twelve years old before she returned to work. We travelled at least once a year, and their hard work allowed me the opportunity to visit several countries from as far east as Thailand, to the Seychelles in the South, and from eastern Europe to as far west as Canada, before we would eventually migrate here. Travelling the world was a rich experience and made me appreciate the diversity of culture and tradition that characterized so many different peoples. Global travel is less common among folks living in North America, save for a minority with the means and resources to do so. It is one of the biggest advantages I felt we enjoyed by living in Dubai, so centrally located on the global stage. My life will always be richer for those experiences, and yet it highlighted constantly the tumultuous nature of social hierarchies. Experiencing life as locals do around the world gave me an appreciation for the complexity inherent in reality, something conspicuously absent in every travel brochure. Then again, travel brochures do not showcase real life for those who call those places home; they provide an idealized version for people looking to escape from their own homes and lives.

A pivotal pitstop on my life journey leading to Canada came in the way of a health crisis. At the age of eleven, I was diagnosed with a hereditary eye disease that could ultimately lead to a complete loss of sight. At the time there did not seem to be any sense of panic; the doctors believed that treatment could wait until my body was done growing. The best estimate back then was that I had until approximately the age of eighteen to twenty-one before this would be a major concern. Life had other plans. By fourteen I had forty-five percent vision in the left eye but only five percent vision in the right. I found myself sitting alone in an ophthalmologist's office having a discussion about what life would be like in a month when I went blind. The doctor explained to me that the cornea in my right eye was so thin that it was at risk of tearing, and when that happened, my retina would get damaged from the exposure. We had a conversation that seemed to last an eternity. I know now from life experience and many visits with doctors that the conversation was probably only a few minutes long in reality. Nonetheless, I sat there listening to his description of what life would be like, and I imagined every way in which my life would never be the same again. I remember thinking that at least I was fortunate to have seen many places in the world, and I would need to cement those memories when my world went dark. The last thing I remember him saying was that he could operate on my eyes once I went blind, because I would have nothing more to lose at that point. A strange notion, and an odd conversation to have with a fourteen-year-old with no adult present. Looking back, that conversation was so lacking. Thousands of people live fulling and rich lives with a whole range of disabilities. This was hardly a death sentence, yet at that stage of life, I could not see the whole picture so clearly. The thoughts in my head as I left the doctor's office were all-consuming, mostly negative, and positively terrifying. I called my parents, who were vacationing in Australia at the time, and gave them the news. We would reconvene as a family in a couple of weeks back in Dubai and explore the options. Up to that point those felt like the longest two weeks of my life. In hindsight it could have been an instructive period that highlighted how easily the mind could get lost in the chaos and the fog of the immediate situation one is dealing with. It would be a lesson I would not learn for decades to come. A couple of weeks later, my family was reunited after summer vacation, and we followed up at a private Russian hospital that had opened up in Dubai after the fall of the former Soviet Union. The surgeon there confirmed that the first doctor was half correct, I was now two weeks away from being blind. However, he was confident that they could perform a successful cornea transplant if only I could get to Moscow immediately.

Russia was an interesting experience, unlike anything I had seen thus far. A translator picked us up at Moscow airport and brought us to the hospital. A sprawling building with all Russian staff but not a single Russian patient visible. My first week there was mostly pre-operation testing, but I had a chance to go see a sliver of this beautifully complex city with a long history. Standing in the middle of Red Square and appreciating the architecture was fascinating and especially meaningful given how I believed that my capacity to see the world could forever be altered by the end of the week if anything did not go as planned. My time in Russia could fill an entire chapter, but for now, I would like to focus on a few key takeaways. I had seen abject poverty many times in my life on my travels, but being up close and personal to it in a new place was humbling all over again. We had rented a room in a building near the hospital for the first week and walked in the neighbourhood to local stores to pick up supplies. The bakery had an extremely long line for day-old bread and almost no one in line for fresh bread. I felt a level of guilt when it appeared that no one else in that store even glanced over at the line I was in. Turns out the fall of communism was not all sunshine and roses for the ordinary person; achieving capitalism and democracy is a slow process and not some utopian silver bullet many are made to believe it is. The family that owned the apartment where we rented the room included a child about my age. That entire week we hung out every evening, playing cards, going for walks with her dog, meeting up with her friends, and sitting around the kitchen table passing the time. The incredible thing was that we could not even speak the same language; she did not understand English and I could not communicate in Russian. We probably had no common life experiences or culture, and yet we found a way to cooperate and coexist in a small space. Just two children who managed to play card games, laugh, and smile without words, connected only by our common humanity and the innocent disposition seemingly unique to youth. Looking back, I appreciate the simplicity of those interactions. We did not think about race, gender, religion, or culture; we were just two kids happy to have some company and willing to find a way to communicate as humans in a shared world. As I would later discover, that was one of the simplest interactions I could have when confronted with new traditions and people in my soon-to-be new home in Canada.

Almost a year later, I had made a slow but positive recovery from my cornea transplants. Our permanent resident visas had come in from the Government of Canada, and we would soon embark on our journey westward towards Ontario to become newly landed immigrants. From all the conversations we had in the days leading up to our move, one would imagine we were finally en route to the land of milk and honey, a place where the inequities of our life in the Middle East would become a distant memory. The stratification of society would be less visible, and most significantly, I would feel welcomed and included in a society I could finally call home. I imagine a lot of new immigrants arrive here with that positive attitude, a yearning for a new beginning and a better life. Yet that utopian ideal is rarely realized, and for some, the experience of being a stranger in a new land is both daunting and disorienting. Contrary to my early perceptions, Ontario was very much a stratified society in the nineties. That period saw a large influx of new immigrants from South East Asia, and with change usually comes resistance. We moved to a predominantly Caucasian neighbourhood, a deliberate decision that we believed would allow us to assimilate into our new home. Much to my surprise, our differences in culture, race, and ethnicity would become a defining feature of my early experiences in Canada. It was here in the mid-nineties that I first encountered the term 'Paki', one I actually did not realize was intended to be derogatory. I remember clarifying for people early on that I was in fact Indian, not Pakistani, while also sharing that people from both those countries shared common ancestry and that the separation of the countries into two autonomous sovereign nations was merely the result of a geo-socio-political divide that came about in the late 1940s when India gained independence from British rule. Nobody back then seemed to care much for my history lesson.

When you grow up in a country mostly comprising your own countrymen, as was the case in the United Arab Emirates, you tend not to focus on your national identity even though you are an expatriate. In Canada, however, I was a stranger and a visible minority, another term that I was previously unfamiliar with but one that would soon become a central feature of my new identity. My attempts at contextualizing history and clarifying my ancestry were often met with a dismissive statement that implied my explanation was a distinction without a difference to those around me. The term 'Paki' as I experienced it was not intended to signify a country of origin but rather the state of being an other, a brown faced other. One who did not belong, a foreigner in someone else's home, a person who was not at home. The old saying about sticks and stones seemed naive; in restaurants and in places of employment I heard a series of comments, directed at me by random strangers, that I had rarely experienced before despite growing up as an expatriate in a country that viewed people like me as 'less than'. Those comments included but were not limited to "Go back to where you came from; get back on the boat; you people come here and take our jobs; this neighbourhood is going downhill now that people like you live here; you refugees are a drain on our country." For obvious reasons, almost all such comments came across as disjointed and factually flawed. I had arrived here as an independent immigrant, not a refugee. Even had I been a refugee, the comment would have seemed odd, given the global view of Canada as a warm, welcoming nation with the friendliest citizens in the world. The idea of our depreciating effect on the local community was equally puzzling; we bought homes with large down payments given our lack of credit history in the country, which actually meant we were very invested in our homes and our community. We shopped there and spent money in the local economy, paid taxes, and did not collect any government subsidies. We paid our dues and took pride in home owner-ship. One would think this would make us ideal new arrivals, people who would contribute and add value, but it turns out the conversation had little to do with economic monetary policy and everything to do with a changing community aesthetic. On the employment front, there seemed to be little advantage being an immigrant. The common line we have all probably heard too often is, "You don't have Canadian experi-ence," an odd statement given the nature of entry level jobs, more perplexing because the jobs I considered at the time were hardly coveted and definitely not in short supply. The larger and not so subtle implication was that workplaces were changing, the shades around them were darkening, the culture was shifting. That made people feel uncomfortable. It also made finding my way in this new land all the more chal-lenging.

The next decade would shape my Canadian identity greatly. It would provide me with a sense of purpose and a career, but the road ahead would hardly be smooth. I entered law enforcement and worked through a variety of positions from protection dog handler to mobile patrol and response, even a short stint in executive protection before entering manage-ment. The early years in law enforcement were tumultuous to navigate. The industry was primarily male and Caucasian, but

I figured fifty percent commonality was a reasonable starting point. The culture was hierarchical and deeply rooted in tradition; I was often referred to as the 'token minority' on the platoon, a direct reference to how noticeably I stood out amongst my peers. Law enforcement tends to lag behind mainstream society in terms of inclusivity and change; that was clearly apparent in the training, the methods of operation, and the jargon that clearly demarcated the 'us' from the 'them.' My experience however was odd because I was simultaneously an 'us' and a 'them'. The people I interacted with treated me with a level of disdain and disappointment, as if I had somehow betrayed my own in favour of a paler fraternity. Yet internally, I would never truly fit into the dominant culture. I was a part of the changing demographic, something to be expected but ostensibly out of place and context. I had been here before, an outsider allowed in but not fully accepted. My time in the Middle East had prepared me for such an experience. Equality was not really a concept I had given much attention, it was not my lived reality. I was raised in a culture that seemed to promote the notion that the world may very well be inherently unfair, but it is the only world we have, and as such it is incumbent upon each of us to find a path forward. Life would eventually become more routine, I would eventually buy a home in the suburbs and travel into the city for work. Ironically the reality I previously described would also be my lived reality in my new neighbourhood. Those early years in Canada seemed to repeat themselves, although this time I knew what it meant to be a strange face in a neighbourhood where I stood out. Through it all, I was still committed to the idea of assimilation. I had come here looking for a place where I would belong, a place to call home. I am patriotic to this country that provided me with a new life. I have a tremendous amount of respect for the Canadian national identity, the flag, the anthem, and the oath I had taken when I became a citizen. I follow the law, pay my taxes, vote in every election, and love being Canadian. Being Canadian means something deeply important to me, so it was always difficult to hear the phrase "where are you really from?" I have been asked that question more times than I care to remember. Embedded in those five words is the constant reminder that I may be here now, but I am not 'from' here, I am an outsider, an immigrant, a guest in someone else's home.

My law enforcement career came to an end when I became a professor at the local community college near where I lived. I became a faculty member with the School of Justice and Emergency Services, a role that would cement my identity to date. Like every experience before it, I stood out and felt different from the moment I walked in the door. I didn't know if this place would give me a sense of finding home, but it had promise. At the time I began my academic career, the student body and definitely the faculty at the college lacked diversity. I soon found myself playing the role of mentor to the few minority students in our programs. It seemed like a daily occurrence to have a student who was either a visible minority or a new immigrant sitting in the extra chair in my office sharing experiences of being 'othered' and being glad to have finally found someone who could relate. This bond between people with like experiences and culture provided me with a sense that I was doing something that mattered. I was able to welcome people to a place where they felt they didn't belong, and I could relate and marshal my experiences to help them navigate theirs. It was a deeply rewarding role, and while it was informal, it was one of the most gratifying periods in my career. Ironically, I would soon become the poster representative for the college; my face was used in marketing materials everywhere on campus. At first I thought it was offensive, a cheap ploy to feign a commitment to diversity. In time I realized it gave people someone to look at who was like them. They could see themselves represented in the space where they wanted to be. Now that I am older, with significantly more grey hair, and not being nearly as much of a novelty, I am no longer featured in the marketing materials. I do not miss it because I interpret it as a sign of progress. I am not novel because the student body and the faculty have become more diverse over the almost two decades I have been there. Students do not need to seek me out as a mentor when they see themselves represented everywhere. They have an easier time finding their way forward. I take pride in having had the opportunity to make a small contribution to their environment. Like so many others before me, I realized that we all have a vital role to play in building community and helping those who come after us find their place in their new home.

Immigration and settlement are shared activities that require grit, resilience, and staying power. It comes with adversity and rejection, but we all play a part in the metamorphosis of our complex society. We did walk out of Africa as one, and after circumnavigating this planet, we became many who prospered and multiplied through mutual cooperation and community. We knew little but adapted constantly. The catalyst for change is often harsh and full of suffering, but that is the human story. Our commitment is to pass on our experiences, our learned wisdom, and our recognition of humanity in everyone. Through it all, people will always seek a path to self-actualization, a journey to find themselves and their place in this complex world. If there is one constant in this existence, it is the human quest to always find the way forward.

As for me, I did find home. My initial perception that home is not necessarily a physical place but rather a state of mind still feels most true to me. A few years ago, I married a woman named Kristen. She comes from a founding family whose members settled the highlands outside of Ottawa many generations and several hundred years ago; I am a first generation Canadian, a newcomer to the land. My journey that began on the other side of the world would ultimately bring me to the most brilliant, intelligent, resilient, and beautiful woman I have ever known. Turns out my immigrant story is a love story, a complex and unlikely union of two people born continents and oceans apart. More than anyone, she is the person who knows me best, who shares the good days and the hard memories with me, with whom my past comes to rest and with whom my future looks so bright. In her presence I live in my present, a place where my skin colour, my ethnicity, my culture, and my being are simply part of our amazing human condition. I have found my person, the one with whom I do not need language all the time, whose kind look and gentle caress as we sit beside each other reading our books and sipping our tea makes me realize that I found home, I found peace and the sense of belonging I spent a lifetime looking for. It has been pointed out that we live in a biracial marriage and share biracial children. I strongly dislike those terms because they put too great an emphasis on a superficial characteristic. Biracial is probably inaccurate anyway, given the nature of human evolution. Multiracial is most likely closer to accurate and yet equally lacking. I would say it this way: I found my favourite human, and we share a beautiful marriage with beautiful children. We bequeath to them our learned wisdom of global perspectives and tales of perseverance, struggle, and travel. We pass on to our children the understanding that skin colour is one of the least significant things we have in common. Our shared humanity makes us kinfolk, our love and commitment make us family, and our shared safe place makes this home. Wherever life takes me, home is always where my heart is, and the promise to always find our way forward together through whatever complexity and chaos life throws our way is my commitment to my soulmate, my best friend, the greatest love of my life... my wife and my last love!

ABOUT THE AUTHOR

Neil Gonsalves

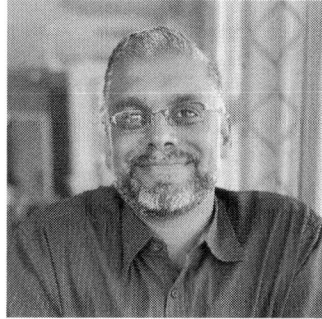

Neil Gonsalves is an educator, public speaker, and training consultant. He has been a community college professor since 2006, teaching primarily in the areas of law enforcement ethics and diversity.

Neil has been a TEDx speaker, a keynoter, and a guest lecturer at several community events. Prior to entering academia, he was the Senior Manager of Staffing and Development for the Toronto branch of a publicly traded security integrator.

He is passionate about fostering an environment that encourages others to share their diverse perspectives and worldviews to promote healthy social discourse.

Connect with Neil Gonsalves:

- Linkedin.com/in/neil-gonsalves-m-ed
- Instagram.com/professorgonsalves

MENTAL HEALTH AND WELLBEING: IS THERE AN ALTERNATIVE WAY?

BY OLESYA KOLISNYK

Good health is in our hands. A statement we hear quite often. However, do we pay attention and give much necessary importance to these words?

Our health is influenced by the environmental, economic, genetic, sociocultural factors, and by our own attitudes and beliefs.

For immigrants, we can add when we immigrated to a new country, where and how we lived previously, and how and why we immigrated. With time, and especially in immigration, our health and well-being tend to become less important. Stress tends to intensify. Going through many sudden changes in our lives—within a relatively short period— is very stressful. Cumulative problems in everyday life, which continue over time, will then surely for many leave marks on our mental health. The nature of the immigration experience—particularly any adversity encountered before, during, or after immigration—heighten the prevalence of mental health problems among immigrants.

. . .

My friend immigrated to Canada in relatively good mental and physical health. Dealing with settlement and changes to her professional career took priority. However, she began to experience sadness because she missed her immediate family and friends from back home. And there was never enough time to meet new friends in Canada. Attending regular religious services helped her to transition to the new country. She felt that she could put on hold her life outside the professional work, until she is caught up and felt established in Canada.

Time flies and tends to make corrections. She experienced changes in her personal life; later, a tragic event happened in her family. Gradually, the occasional sadness she experienced at the beginning grew over time into a major depressive disorder with a form of psychosis not yet defined in the diagnostic manual.

Pharmacological interventions secured her capacity to take care of basic needs. However, they put a hold on her growth and development as an individual for an indefinite time—if the right treatment modality is found.

How did all this happen? Mental health problems might become evident at the beginning or reveal themselves later in life in various manifestations. As we can learn, Immigrants are less likely than the general population to seek out or be referred to mental health services—compared to native residents—even when they experience similar levels of distress.[1]

Back home, my friend was outgoing and well socially connected. She became accomplished and quite successful in her professional career in Canada, but during her time of illness, numerous attempts to invite her out failed. She granted me occasional visitations and brief conversations over the phone.

Although I am a healthcare professional myself, when I talked to my friend I did not know what to do or how I could help her. Somehow, I could sense her desire to get better and have a good life. Yet, in the dark moments, we did not have answers about what to do and how.

A traditional health care approach was helpful but not sufficiently so. Immigrants are disruptive individuals who tend to question the status quo and challenge the traditional approaches, just as they did when they decided to leave their homeland. Despite numerous pieces of advice from friends and family to stay, most immigrants take a one-way ticket to another country for various reasons. As immigrants, we have a certain strength within us—it is crucial, and it is our driving force for making a change.

Immigration is a change. And "the secret of change," as Socrates taught us, "is to focus all your energy, not on fighting the old, but on building the new."[2]

Focusing attention predominantly on work and overlooking the importance of social and physical aspects of human nature brought my friend's life to a significant turning point. Life made her pause, think, and decide.

There were two possible directions. One was a reliance on medications, where all her strength would be spent on enduring side effects and functioning at a very basic level. We did not know for sure whether there was a second direction but wanted to believe there was a brighter alternative. So, the second choice was the decision. This unknown path had the potential to lead us to a recovery, in which she could function at a significantly better level than with taking medications. This was our common goal, to win the battle with the illness.

Meantime, I came across a yoga philosophy postulating that we have what it takes to succeed. All we need is to find a balance between physical, mental, and emotional energy to reach our utmost inner potential. I became curious. And when yet another acute psychotic episode subsided, I encouraged my friend to rethink her approach based on what was important to her. Because how she approached life until this point, and her behaviours thus far, did not serve her well. To me, it was almost as if her body and mind were calling for help and asking for a change.

Since she immigrated, there might have been numerous times when her body alerted her to pay closer attention to its needs. But she might have disregarded those symptoms and manifestations because she was preoccupied with her career, volunteering, and family needs. The time for a change was now.

I thought that if she could work to find the balance in physical, mental, and emotional energies within herself, there would be a chance of her mind healing. I did not know how much time this process will take. And we did not find an answer in any literature.

I believe that immigrants have a lot of strength and determination to guide their journey in the new country. As immigrants, we need to find the courage to accept that, sometimes, the grass might not necessarily be greener in the new country. Acceptance and a possible change in perception could be a start towards healing.

My immigrant friend's strength included also a strong desire to live a fulfilling and meaningful life, and this should have helped her to deal with these mental health challenges.

Numerous factors influence our mental health and wellbeing. Biomedicine and relevant science focus on helping us understand better the existence of a problem. However, we might also notice how the more we focus on scientific rationales for mental health issues, the more our mind tends to gravitate towards and rely on solutions with anecdotal evidence and explanations. Carl Jung suggested that the modern man is overwhelmed and is in search of a soul.

As a first step in her recovery journey, my friend relied on her strong religious side. Regular church attendance was very important to her so making a conscious, if laboured, effort to get up, get ready, and come to church was a start. She used to run and exercise in a gym before the illness manifested. But now, she did not have the strength to resume these activities on her own. She needed support, encouragement, and guidance to stay on track.

Yoga was a new approach. I asked her to join a trial session to see how she felt there. I like yoga, especially the final pose, Shavasana, which is lying down and doing nothing. Every yoga instructor says it is the most important pose. Where else do we hear that lying down and doing nothing is the most important aspect of practice?

For my friend, falling and getting up numerous times and turning in the wrong direction because her left and right legs and hands were not coordinating was an immediate reaction. But overall, she liked the trial session and signed up for a membership. She attended basic level classes as a beginner. There were yogis in the room with an instructor, and they did not know she was ill. The instructor would guide the participants, help with poses, and encourage an appropriate pace. As a result, she became motivated to go to the studio three to four times a week. She would practice and have some social interaction there. The first signs of "normalcy"—where she would not think and talk about the illness—became evident within two months. I noticed she paid more attention to her diet and started to lose weight. We then had much longer conversations, and she would smile again and have a sparkle in her eyes.

Literature suggests that our success comes from our grit, which in turn comes from the passion for what we do and our perseverance over a long period. My friend had to be disciplined, consistent, and determined in this process to attain positive and sustainable results on the road to mental wellness.

The stigma associated with mental health is one of the most important factors preventing immigrants from seeking help.[3] Mental health problems are frequently viewed as a source of shame and embarrassment for both the individual and the family. As a result, such mental health problems often remain unacknowledged. In many cases, individuals look for culturally appropriate ways to express their psychological distress. For example, people might somatize their psychological distress and talk about it by describing physical symptoms. These symptoms could be fatigue, pain, nausea, shortness of breath, muscle weakness, or several others. In many cultures, physical symptoms such as these are less stigmatizing than psychological symptoms, such as bouts of crying, suicidal thoughts, and panic attacks[1].

Understanding the stigma and its implications alone did not help my friend in sharing her mental health struggles and seeking help early. Hiding the problem and fighting alone was what she did early on. She believed that mental health problems should be overcome on one's own.

Indeed, cultural values within many immigrant communities promote a strong sense of self-reliance and a high degree of family cohesiveness. However, these values prevent them from seeking appropriate professional help promptly.

Taking action was useful for my friend at the beginning. However, it predisposed her to many severe problems later on. Her symptoms did not go away, and she could carry on only for so long on her own in fighting the battle.

Research has shown that when human cells are isolated, they begin to act chaotically and destructively. But when human cells act together, they fight viruses and diseases more effectively. Similarly, on a macro level, we as humans need allies to face life challenges.

We were together and very motivated for her full recovery. Significant improvements happened in less than one year. Regular exercise, resuming her hobbies, and becoming more socially present and active helped my friend to return to her previous professional responsibilities at full capacity. In the following year, she said that she felt much better. Almost two years later, we thought we won. It was so worth it not to give up, to seek support, to search for answers, and to try something new. We were happy and very proud.

Seeing my friend recover was the best reward I could have imagined. I am glad to have played a role in her journey. Together, we made a difference to save a life.

Social interactions are of vital importance in maintaining our mental wellbeing. For immigrants, however, shyness and language barriers including accents might hinder interaction with others. Such barriers predispose to loneliness and social isolation. My friend's English skills were advanced, but she was preoccupied with her professional career. It left her little to no time to develop and maintain a socially active lifestyle like the one she had back home. She had limited social interactions, with very few people, for a long time before her illness.

Our longevity, physical and mental health, and happiness are influenced by our social life. Susan Pinker shared—in her 2017 TED talk *The secret to living longer may be your social life*—that the main predictors of how long one is going to live are close relationships and social integration. Close relationships are what you have with people you can talk to at times of existential crisis or people who will take you to the hospital when you are unwell. Social integration, considered the most important factor, reflects how much social interaction we have during a day (how many people we talk to as our day unfolds). For example, Susan Pinker points to talking with a coffee barista, a postman, and with people on the streets. Similarly, Dr. Robert Waldinger shared—in his 2015 TED talk *What makes a good life?*—that good relationships matter because they keep people happy and healthy. Our social connections with family, friends, and community protect our health, physical and mental. Loneliness, on the other hand, is detrimental. A good life is built with good relationships. So it is important to stay socially active and communicate with people to build meaningful, positive, and good relationships and to live longer, healthier, and happier lives.

Staying physically active, adopting healthy eating habits, getting sufficient and good quality sleep, and adopting stress reduction techniques will protect and improve our physical and mental health as well as our overall wellbeing.

As immigrants, we need to be open to and accept change, realign our values, and embrace our new identity in the new country. We need to set realistic goals for ourselves. It is important in our life journey to find a balance between letting go and accepting discomfort.

Identify new ways of doing things. Give ourselves grace and acknowledge that not everything has to fall into place at the same time.

Most immigrants found a way to follow their ambitions and dreams; hence, they chose the new country where they intended to thrive. Even if emigration is not the first choice, people can make relocation work very well for them. To build a successful path in the new country, however, it is crucial to make good decisions by being attuned to our bodies and to anything that resonates with being a human.

My friend learned in a hard way the importance of finding a balance between the social, professional, and personal aspects of her life—by being aware of human needs in mental, physical, and emotional realms. It was a good lesson for both of us.

People have a tendency to take things for granted. Nonetheless, life often teaches us valuable lessons.

In March 2020, within a week, we were in lockdown. What a change! How unexpectedly did it happen? The COVID-19 pandemic interfered in every area and without asking permission to do so. The incorporation of technology into our professional and personal lives was already on the rise before the pandemic; the relatively steady adoption of technological advancements was present in every profession, calling us to work more online or remotely via technology. It amazed me now how fast we all became more technologically savvy during the pandemic. We were not so fast before. How did we learn so quickly? How did we become so creative and adaptable in those two years?

Every country became an "immigrant" in the new pandemic world. There was some emergency preparedness for this, but much was learned in the adaptation process. We were united as humans and determined to win this battle. And we did.

Everybody made a significant contribution to the process as leaders and followers. While the virus originated in China, the solution came in the form of a vaccine created via unprecedented collaboration— between science, medicine, multinational pharmaceutical companies, and governments—to protect us. It shows that there is a balance in the world. And when we unite our efforts, we win.

I wish we could have a balance and be united in the world to restore democracy, peace, and freedom in every country. It is vital to maintain relationships and deal with emergencies or problems as a community. During the pandemic, the global community took action, and every person benefited as a result. We saved lives and humanity in two years.

The consequences of this pandemic are what we are dealing with now. Big cities acquired big problems from an economic standpoint. Higher inflation and interest rates influence all of us.

How about our mental health? Although social interaction is very important for us as humans, for two years we were forced to be in solitude.

The changes to our mental health—and how we dealt with it during the pandemic—impacted almost everyone, even those who did not have mental health problems previously.

Before the pandemic, my friend and I celebrated two years of stability in her condition. We had so many plans for the future. However, when the pandemic started, the yoga studio closed as did many other businesses out there.

My friend worked from home, and for six months, she continued to practice yoga with online instructors. After that, she gradually reduced the time for yoga and slipped onto her couch with almost no physical activity. The new normal—being constantly at home and taking a daily walk in the city—became the routine. We connected via technology for some social time with our friends. Slowly we did less. It hit me and it hit her.

After a year and a half, the sadness, depression, and psychosis reappeared for her. From outside, it was hard to know that. We did so much and worked so hard to get better. In an acute state, she was admitted to the hospital. That helped. But when she was discharged and returned to isolation at home, there was very little progress. She was readmitted a few times, and the former trajectory repeated itself for her. It seemed unfair, but that was the reality.

Meantime, there was progress in fighting the COVID-19 virus and its variants. The restrictions and isolation requirements slowly lifted. We continued to wear masks and started to be outside more often. Businesses were allowed to open. Gradually we started to come out without masks and see each other's faces again.

We had to re-learn that an elevator can hold more than two people and that you may talk to people while in the elevator. It is ok to stand closer to each other in a line-up. There were no more markings on the floor or on the seats in public transit to stay 6 ft apart.

And if somebody coughs, COVID-19 was a possibility. But there are many other reasons for coughing to happen. It is good to know that every person now knows how to wash hands properly and understands how important it is for our health and safety. Unfortunately, it had to take a pandemic for that—prior public health efforts were not as successful.

It was a point of celebration to know that summer festivals will resume. There was so much hope for all of us to get back to "normal" life.

Although my friend relapsed, this time we knew that there is a way to recover. It was not a question of whether and how she got better, but a matter of how quickly she could resume her previous activities.

When things started to open, her route to recovery started with church, yoga studio, nature walks, and visiting every friend we knew. Yes, it was in-person visiting. We had had enough phone and video calls during two years. My friend attended every festival and started numerous volunteer activities she would not have done prior to the pandemic.

Everybody was hungry for social interaction, but for her, it was also critically important to get better. This time, she bounced back much faster because she knew how and what she had to do. In a few months, we celebrated positive progress in her mental wellness.

While people in the community slowly got back to "normal" after COVID-19, my friend realized how much she values life and made a decision: to restart her life as if she never had this illness before. It seems she needed this valuable lesson.

The very same walks she took before were now filled with brighter colours. And the water in the lake was more beautiful every time she saw it. Each time she spoke to me about nature, the sky, and the forest, it was as if she had seen them for the first time.

The return to "normal" was different for each of us. Quite frankly, I do not think we will ever be the same as before COVID-19. We are much wiser and stronger, and we care for each other so much more now. Gradually we become social again, some faster than others. We dive into different activities, putting on masks when we hear an emergency warning about a spike in some COVID-19 variant, and washing our hands.

The fear of possible lockdowns might still be present in our minds, which makes us more responsible and vigilant about how to prevent the wider spread of the virus.

Mental health challenges touched many during these days in various ways. Mental wellness became a higher priority for all of us. We had time to reflect during those two years and think about what we wanted to do after the lockdown, and whether we needed to do things differently.

Life is a journey on which we learn, grow, and discover ourselves. Sometimes life gives us valuable lessons to help us appreciate our life and evolve to be better humans.

I think life took my friend on a journey where she re-evaluated herself, her role, her priorities, her focus, and—for sure—the importance of holistic health and the meaning of true friendship and of all the other things we so often take for granted: nature, our environment, the importance of interacting with each other, our ingenuity, the role of community, time spent together, and our presence in the world as humans.

We are much stronger when we are united in our efforts to make a positive change in the world. Let's remember the lessons we learned.

1
Informed Immigrant, 2022: "Mental Health for Immigrants: Taking. Care of yourself & loved ones." https://informedimmigrant.com/guides/mental-health-undocumented-immigrants/
2
Philosophy and Psychology, 2020: "5 Great Lessons from Socrates' Life."
https://exploringyourmind.com/5-great-lessons-socrates-life/
3
Mental Health Commission of Canada, 2022: "Stigma and Discrimination."
https://mentalhealthcommission.ca/what-we-do/stigma-and-discrimination/

ABOUT THE AUTHOR

Olesya Kolisnyk

Olesya Kolisnyk emigrated from Ukraine in 2002. Being an educator, she transitioned into an academic role in Canada and is a PhD candidate.

As a registered nurse, Olesya has helped people overcome physical and psychological illnesses to reach their optimal state of wellbeing.

As a professor, she is nurturing the development of a new generation of nurses, supporting students in accomplishing their dreams of entering professional nursing practice.

As a researcher, she contributes to advancements in international nursing education in countries with emerging economies.

Olesya serves as an IWA Board member and is the organizer for TEDxTrinityBellwood events in Toronto.

Connect with Olesya Kolisnyk:

- Linkedin.com/in/olesya-kolisnyk

A JOURNEY TO REMEMBER

BY RAMONA VIZITIU

I found a way.

It's an uphill path to the top of the mountain. It's not going to be easy for me; the sun will burn me, the rain will make me shiver, the snow will freeze me, and the spring season will warm me up. My feet will have bruises, my legs will hurt. I will go on. I must go on. I must reach the top of the mountain.

Two years ago, I was climbing the same mountain, but on a different path. It was so easy. It was always warm, the sun caressed me, there were barely a few drops of rain, and it was never cold. At night I would rest peacefully, excited for the next day's adventure. I was happy until the day the great big storm came. Monstrous. Unstoppable. It threw me down to the base of the mountain. The wind didn't stop. I rolled down crying, scared, and hurt until I reached the bottom of the sea. I yelled for help until my heart stopped.

I was born in communist Romania in 1981. I had a beautiful life there despite all the challenges. I was lucky to have a loving family, a good financial situation, and all the things I wished for. I never fit in there though. I have had a love for the

English language since I was little, and I asked my parents to give me as many private English lessons as they could afford. When I was in grade four, I told my father that I wanted to live in a country where English was the official language. I believe in a soul plan. I believe there are no coincidences. My father got a phone call one day that led to our immigration to Canada when I was 25 years old. I couldn't have been happier. Finally, I had made it where I was supposed to be! I love my birth country, but I love it like a dear friend I left behind on my way to meeting the friend I was going to live with for the rest of my life. I was finally home. In Canada, I felt free to live my life the way I wanted to. I no longer felt stuck, imprisoned by beliefs and moral values that did not align with mine.

My life in beautiful Canada unfolded. I had a wonderful husband, two amazing daughters, my parents close by, wonderful new friends, and a successful career in law. I integrated right away into the community. Everything was perfect, all challenges were welcome, and all successes were uplifting. I was rich, not financially but spiritually. I was proud. More than proud, I was vain. My ego was the size of a castle.

And then the great big storm hit.

On January 5, 2020, we welcomed in our life another miracle. Her name was Mia. Beautiful Mia. We waited so long for her to complete our family. We were bursting with happiness.

I will never forget the image of Mia resting peacefully in her little white coffin. At that moment in time, my heart stopped.

On February 7, 2020, a month after she was born, Mia spread her angel wings and left this world.

I did not want to live. I did not accept the reality of what happened.

I don't believe in Hell as a place where God punishes her children by throwing them in fire. That is ridiculous in my view. God is love. And we are God's children. How could she punish her own children?

I do believe though in Hell on Earth. And I do believe in Heaven on Earth. I lived both at the same time. Mia was with me on Earth for thirty-four days. Her life was full of suffering, with glimpses of relief. I cried with her, and I laughed with her. I held her tight, and I had to let her go. I sang her songs, and I watched her die. I went through Heaven and Hell in a roller coaster of emotions.

On a spiritual level, I have found hope. I found the way. I want to write this in big letters so that all mothers who have lost a child can see it. I want to shout at the top of my lungs that our children are still alive. And they are very much still here. Energy never dies.

I am on a journey. I am following my soul plan. Long before I became a mother, my soul was preparing me for what was coming. In a reading room on the main floor of a residential building, there were a few books on a shelf left by their previous owners for anyone to take home. I browsed through them, and I found only one of interest. It called me. It was a blue book with the title "Broken Open." The subtitle was "How difficult times can help us grow." The author is Elizabeth Lesser. Even though the title was a little dark, it intrigued me. I picked it up and took it home, but did not touch it for more than 10 years.

Not long after Mia transitioned, I saw the book in my bookcase, and I started reading it. I gasped when I reached the chapter that was waiting patiently for me, remembering how long it has been since I got the book. The chapter was entitled "No birth, no death." It talks about the teachings of the Vietnamese Zen monk Thich Nhat Hanh. Right there, in that moment, my heart started beating again, about six months after Mia's passing.

I devoured this chapter with the hunger of a starving animal deprived of food for months. The monk talks about how death is perceived in our minds. When we think of death, the thought that comes to mind is that we become no-one. We no longer exist. We also think of birth as a beginning. We believe that when we are born, we come here from nothing. From nothing, you become something. From no-one, you become someone. This belief is the root of a fear deep within us. Buddha discovered something different: no birth and no death. It annihilates our fear of dying. Nothing is born, nothing can die. What does a birth certificate say? We started existing on this particular day. Yet, we know that we existed even before that, in the womb of our mothers. And even before the day we were conceived, we were there, in our mother, father, in our ancestors, and everywhere else. You can try to go back, but you will not find a beginning of you.

The monk gives an example of a sheet of paper. We think that one day, that sheet of paper was produced from nothing, only to become something. The truth is, when we touch the paper, we touch the tree that the paper was made from, we touch the sunshine. We touch the cloud that gave rain to allow the tree to grow. We touch the minerals of the Earth, the Earth herself, time, space, people, and insects. The same applies to our bodies.

If we burn the piece of paper, we see ashes falling on the ground, and smoke going up in the sky. It has become a part of the cloud in the sky, and it has returned to earth. The paper may touch you again in the form of a raindrop, or in the form of a new leaf in a tree, although you may not be aware that it's the same sheet of paper.

By the same principle, our bodies are not us. Our eyes are not us. Identifying with this lifespan is wrong. It is an illusion to imagine that we are separated from anything else in space or time. We are everything at the same time.

I took my first breath after long months of barely living.

Two years after Mia left, I am here. Alive. Telling you our story. I didn't outlive her. She never died. Mia is alive. I do not have to be on Earth without Mia. Mia did not leave me. Her physical body died, but her spirit was liberated and returned home.

It took a great amount of psychotherapy and lots of support from my family and friends to keep me going. I never intended to commit suicide, but I died inside. I was a living corpse. I was moving and doing things in a lifeless manner.

Traditional therapy, antidepressants, and grief support groups did not help. I was desperately looking for help. "Please God, I need something to save me."

You know, there are angels on Earth. They are walking around us and they are saving people every day.

I met my angel Claudia almost a year after Mia transitioned. When I met her, I was without hope that I could ever smile and enjoy life again. Something struck me. Her beautiful daughter Emma had transitioned as well, but Claudia still had life in her. She had the kindest voice, and I was blown away that she was still smiling.

Claudia knew. I didn't know. Our girls were alive. They just went home.

Following in Claudia's steps, I joined Helping Parents Heal, a non-profit organization dedicated to assisting bereaved parents. They "go a step beyond other groups by allowing the open discussion of spiritual experiences and evidence for the afterlife, in a non-dogmatic way." The mothers there welcomed me with open arms. This group has become my new hope, my new family, my new path.

I discovered healing through writing. At first, I wrote to Mia. Then she wrote back through me. Then I wrote our story. Then I wrote her a letter for Christmas. It's painful. It's enlightening. It's divine. It's healing.

Two years after Mia passed, I am still grieving. I am not completely healed, and I will never be. The human in me will never stop missing baby Mia. I will never stop wishing that this was all a bad dream, that Mia is walking and talking, is hugging me, and is enjoying life on Earth with us. I am grieving the steps not taken, the words not spoken, the laughter not laughed. I will take those steps instead. I will speak those words. I will laugh that laughter. I will be her voice. Mia lives through me and I live through her. We are one. We are taking this journey together.

The soul in me has found peace. I was reborn. I burned to ashes and came back a different person.

I have more patience with people and I am more compassionate with respect to other people's challenges. I met incredible mothers since Mia's transitioning; their support has been life-saving, and their strength and hope have been uplifting.

I started a non-profit organization together with two other mothers. It provides non-traditional grief support for bereaved mothers in the Toronto area.

I rediscovered my passion for writing. This is the third book I am co-authoring, and I am in addition writing a book on my own. Each time I write, I heal.

I look at life differently now. I realize that living without a purpose is living an empty life. I realize that life is precious and that we shouldn't take our next breath for granted.

I found a way. I will get to the top of the mountain, where my daughter is patiently waiting for me. The sun will burn me, the rain will make me shiver, and the snow will freeze me. But also, the spring season will warm me up. On my way up, I will take in the beauty of the world and breathe deeply. I will cherish every breath I take and every moment I spend with my two living daughters. When the wind blows, I will tell it to blow from the back, so I can rise higher. When the rain pours, I will take it as a blessing as I will have drinking water to survive. When the snow freezes me, I will look for shelter in warm arms and rest until the storm goes away.

I will be one with Mother Earth, all the way to the top of her highest mountain. And when I get to the top, Mia will gently whisper to me: "Welcome home, mom. Rest in my arms. We had quite the journey."

ABOUT THE AUTHOR

Ramona Vizitiu

Born and raised in Romania, Ramona Vizitiu moved to Canada at the age of 25. Here she continued her career in the legal field for 11 more years until her life took a dramatic turn following the transition of her baby Mia.

Ramona lives in Toronto with her two other beautiful daughters, Arianna and Sonia, and her husband, Eugen.

She has a passion for reading, writing, and photography.

Since her daughter transitioned, Ramona's life radically changed. Together with other mothers, she started the non-profit organization *Shining in the Light of Our Kids*—which offers support group meetings for bereaved mothers in the Toronto area.

Connect with Ramona Vizitiu:

- Amazon.com/author/ramona.vizitiu
- About.me/ramonavizitiu

THE WAY FORWARD

BY PAUL LEBEDEV

While the Russian president was enjoying his palace, Vlad and his parents were rushing to the nearest access point.

Access points allowed faster travel between different countries and cities. There was no immediate prospect of change in Russia. The drive proved a slow, stop-and-start affair. Vlad looked out of the car window, attempting to visualize Toronto. That's where he was going. His father had asked him once at a movie theatre whether he wanted to go to Canada. He'd said yes without ever having been in that country before. In his mind, it was like America. America was somewhat familiar. He imagined suburbs: luscious green lawns, nearly identical houses, dogs prancing and yapping, small rainbows brought to life by spinning sprinklers, and a giant mall. That was the only picture of Canada that he had inside his mind, and it did not look bad at all.

Yes, that felt like a place where he would like to be, rather than Moscow with its exhaust fumes that coloured the sky brown and the sour, grim expressions that people wore like proofs of the general state of disrepair, both of the infrastructure and the government—as well as the people themselves, their grieving souls.

The family of three hurriedly walked down the resounding marble hallways, waited in seemingly interminable lines, and prepared to make their final journey.

"Remember, Vlad," his father said with his hands on the boy's shoulders and his breath smelling of cigarettes, "once we enter Layer One, we must go straight to the access point marked 'Toronto.' Do not, under any circumstances, leave the marked path."

"Okay," the boy said. There was something comforting about his father's smell, as if the clinging cigarette smoke was an indication of where home was. His father was home.

"You heard me, right? We might not see each other on the other side. Not until we're in Toronto. The other Layers are weird and not like our world."

"Okay."

A green light lit up high on the opposite wall. In the centre of the room, on the floor, a disc lit up like an enormous brown coin. Vlad then observed a man who was dressed in black and whose eyes shone with a golden tint. "Who's that?" Vlad asked. The man looked strange, like no man he'd ever seen, an inexplicable phenomenon, like a lightning bolt in a blue sky.

"He's a morgud," his father answered. "Morguds come from Layer One. They gave us access to Layer One. We're technically Layer Zero, the basest one of all." His father chuckled ruefully.

"But why? Why did they give us access?"

"Apparently, they established relations with all the other Layers first. Before our turn came. They said it's because they want to create unity among all the Layers. A single unified reality. It seems, though, that they're the only ones willing to engage with us so far." His father chuckled again, with the same ruefulness. "They're idealists."

The line shuffled forward. One by one, people stepped onto the glowing disc and vanished. Vlad's mother remained silent. She was not prone to wasting words. He was always afraid of upsetting her with his words, always waiting for her to say that his remark was stupid or not thought through, yet underneath that sharpness and strictness of speech, he knew that she meant well.

Vlad stepped into the white light. Just before he moved into the other Layer, he saw the golden eyes of the man in black. Then Vlad opened his eyes to behold a path of white light that wound its way among black hills strewn with brown boulders. The boulders resembled giant crumpled balls of paper. They lay under an ashen grey sky. In several places, yellow gashes revealed the insides of the hills. From most of those yellow gashes, bones protruded, brown ones. As Vlad walked along the path, reminding himself over and over again to stay on it—he appeared to be utterly alone—he could not help eyeing the bones. They were all different shapes and sizes. He believed that he could recognize some as being leg bones or shoulder bones, arm bones, or ribs. What sorts of creatures did they belong to? They were clearly ancient. Everything was so weird here, so unlike real life. He couldn't believe it. There had been only a handful of times when he'd been so disoriented during a journey, and that was when they were driving around America, visiting people he knew only vaguely, having half-remembered conversations. America had felt so large, Canada felt unknown except for that made-up image of suburbia, and Russia was receding quickly, like wind-blown smoke. The colours spun, and his mind wavered and lost its anchor, its grounding. He'd gotten lost in transition, not knowing which way north was anymore or anything else.

As he walked along the path, he did not see the word 'Toronto' anywhere. The path wound among more black hills with more yellow gashes and fossil deposits. A river cut across the path. The river carried slushy ice, and he realized for the first time how cold the air was here. Moving via Layers was supposed to be faster than any method of travel yet invented by humans, but it filled him with leaden dread.

A narrow wooden bridge—about as wide as his pelvis —spanned the river. As he started walking across it, slushy ice suddenly built up against the side of it. Before he had a chance to react, the built-up ice overpowered the bridge, and he got washed away by the river.

He fought for air as the rapid current carried him farther and farther away from his intended destination. He felt like crying. He'd let his parents down, let everybody down, even the man with the bright golden eyes. How could he have messed up so quickly and so badly? The water was freezing cold. Luckily, he slammed into the exposed roots of a tree that grew by the side of the river—and was able to hold onto them. Finally, he did something right during this confusing journey. Just when his life was about to change, he'd lost his compass of reality. Where was he? He was completely lost and utterly confused. Nothing made sense. What was Moscow? What was America? What was Toronto? What was this land, this strange in-between land? His mind reeled and flew away into other dimensions.

He coughed and spat out water while clinging to the roots, even as the river rushed with nearly overpowering speed. Then he changed his grip, one hand at a time, and hoisted himself onto the shore.

Well, that was it. He'd officially messed up. They'd deceived him. They'd mumbled something about Toronto. There was no Toronto. He had no idea where he was, and there was no sign of a path or of an access point marked Toronto. They'd lied. They'd made him confused. They'd uprooted him and thrown him into this dark land.

He wept with a quiet hiccupping hee-hee sound, his eyes closed, the back of his hand placed against his forehead, as if feeling the solid thickness of bone that defined his forehead would help ground him. He had to get this grief out of his system now, before he did anything else. His father's warnings echoed in his mind, a nagging reminder of his failure that was really their failure. They'd abandoned him here, alone and detached from every anchor, every semblance of a home or a direction.

He headed upstream. The river shone a ghostly white, edged with leafless trees and lifeless grass. Black sand lay under his feet. It appeared that only the surface of the sand was black. When he churned the sand this way and that, a yellow underside revealed itself. It made sense that the hills were black on the surface and yellow inside, like the sand underfoot. The wind blew, rippling his clothes, ruffling his dark blond hair. He rubbed his nose as if eliminating an invisible irritant and made the long, slow way back.

Then he heard the screeching of a bird overhead. It sounded like a bird—a seagull. He looked up and saw, instead of a seagull, a reptilian creature with wings on both its arms and its legs, the feathers spread out, colourful and iridescent, while fuzzier and more primitive feathers grew out of the scales on its elongated torso. Its head was triangular and riddled with short yellow horns. Two yellow eyes looked at him. They were positioned in such a way that they could see both in front and to the side, and the flying creature emitted another screech as it swooped down.

It looked as though he would get devoured before he ever reached home.

Where was he going? His mind was divided against itself. The bird looked the way he felt, panicked, confused, disoriented, not knowing his place in the world, not knowing whether he was Russian or Canadian or something else entirely, something in transition, something caught in overly bright headlights, blinded and thrown out of its previous sense of self.

Vlad ran around the nearest black hill. His sneakers laid bare the yellow sand underneath the black surface. The protruding bones that he saw in every yellow gash in the slopes of the hills called to him, inviting him to stop and examine them. The flying reptile had already clenched his T-shirt in its jaws. The monster flapped all four wings as it pulled at him.

The winged reptile sank its talons into his T-shirt—but, fortunately, not his flesh—and raised him a few feet off the ground. His stomach dropped away. He felt hollowed out and queasy, on the verge of expelling his breakfast. Meanwhile, the monster wobbled in the air, apparently unable to carry his weight, and got pulled down into a tree with bare grasping branches, unable to avoid it in time. Vlad swung against the gnarled trunk, his arms wrapping around it through the force of inertia while the side of his face acquired the imprint of the bark's rough and furrowed texture. While that went on, the reptile battled the spreading candelabrum of the branches, as though the branches were actively trying to grab it. It was a pathetic sight, one he didn't get to enjoy as fully as he would've liked, given that he was just then sliding onto the ground and collapsing into a limp heap.

His scalp grew tight and uncomfortable. He got up. Then he almost lost his balance and abruptly changed the position of one foot to keep himself from falling. The creature was just then wresting itself out of the branches and screeching as it did so. He must hurry.

For a while, he jogged along, keeping the river on his right. The hills were numerous. Unable to stifle his curiosity, he peered at a bone that protruded out of one yellow scar of earth. It was a beautiful sight. The bone was curved like a musical instrument. He dug at the earth all around it until he was able to free the bone.

In the distance, the reptile was flapping its four wings again, chasing after him. He would defend himself with the fossil. The bone was a long one, and he would swing it like a sword. His headache worsened by the second, as if some noxious gas was filling his lungs.

The flapping grew audible. The motion of the four limbs with the four wings attached was hypnotizing, like a spinning black-and-white spiral. Yet he stood poised with the bone held like a baseball bat, ready to take a swing.

He wanted to be out of there, not wasting time on battling monsters. His parents had thrown him into a den of wolves. As the creature swooped down, Vlad swung at it just like a hitter in baseball. The bone connected with the upper left wing, and the creature spun counterclockwise, wrapping itself around him, snapping at him with its toothy jaws. They fell backward, and he stuck the bone into the meatiest portion of the beast, its torso. He pushed and pushed until the fossil punched through the flesh and released a flood of green blood. Then he liberated himself from the writhing monster and ran away, leaving his weapon behind, trying to ignore the desperate squawking.

Then, by some miracle, he stumbled onto the white path again. The word 'Toronto' hovered ahead, next to a black hill, surrounded by a white halo. He walked toward it, squinting with suspicion. This was a lie. This was a deception. This was some trick of perception, some shift. His parents had railed against corruption and everything else that was going on in Russia. Everything he knew, he learned from them, even when it was not what everyone else around him believed. They were his guiding star, but now, as his sense of reality flickered unsteadily, his mind lost itself amid all the vastly different environments, and he knew his parents to have been duplicitous. There'd been signs before, signs and signals in the air that he'd ignored. Now, the collision of realities was undeniable.

Several wings flapped in the air. Their flaps were noisy. Claws closed around his arms and lifted him into the air. Two reptiles, similar to the first one, dashed him against the top of yet another hill. Fortunately, he fell next to a boulder rather than on top of it. His mind was running away from the situation, leaving his conscious self, his "I," stranded in a sea of disorientation. He just let things happen to him as the creatures descended and pecked at him. Their teeth sank into him.

That was when a man in black appeared—another morgud —his eyes shining golden in the smoky air. He shooed the monsters away and carried Vlad toward the shining access point.

Then they were out of the blinding glare and in a room where his parents stood with wide eyes and gaping mouths. They rushed over and gathered him up in their arms and buried him with their questions. "What happened? You took so long! We thought you were gone!"

Vlad did not respond. He just grinned at them, smiled at them, the orchestrators of all that madness.

"Let's go," his father said.

They never mentioned that they were in Toronto. This was absolute proof of their deception. They weren't even in Toronto. They were in a dark land of the morguds, disguised as something else. This was all an illusion. He hid his ideas, did not voice them, because he knew that they would try to argue him out of it. They were his enemies.

The family left the building where the access point was housed and entered the parking lot of a car rental, after which point his father drove them into deeply unfamiliar territory. All these people on the streets were morguds. There was no brown haze of exhaust fumes immediately visible in the sky, and there were people of many different ethnic origins on the streets. Back in Moscow, there had been people of different ethnic origins, but they were mostly Central Asians and ethnic Russians. Everyone here was a morgud. They were just wearing civilian clothes, pretending to be Torontonians.

The family arrived at an apartment building beside a park. After settling in one apartment, the three of them went for a walk in the park where roses bloomed and neat rectilinear pathways divided up the grounds. A pond lay in the park, reflecting the dour sky and the massed green leaves and needles of nearby maples and evergreens. The new land was unlike anything he'd ever seen in Russia. At thirteen years old, his whole life and his mind had flipped in a matter of hours, and the absolute, unshakable certainty that he was still in the land with morguds and bird-like creatures was upon him. How could so many different places exist at the same time in almost the same place? They'd deceived him. He clenched his fist.

They did not look at him for some time. He kept trailing behind them, pausing now and then in the hope that a deep gulp of fresh air, tinged with the fragrance of flowers, would ease the blossoming pain inside his head.

"Are you okay?"

"Fine," Vlad replied in a low voice.

"You must've spent too much time in Layer One," his father observed with a frown. Vlad did not mention the bites or the attacks or the fact that they were still in Layer One! The sun dimmed behind a passing cloud that appeared ragged at the edges like the fraying sail of a pirate ship.

They resumed their walk, reaching an affluent neighbourhood of gabled houses and tall trees and vast back yards on a series of green hills. Vlad was once again aghast at the lifestyle before his eyes, which was unlike anything he'd ever seen in Russia.

Evening air entered Vlad's lungs like a series of knives. His vision grew crimson. The peacefulness of the park and the affluent neighbourhood beyond it paled before the growing presence of something alien inside his mind.

They returned to the apartment. His father got them a pizza, and they ate it in silence. Vlad kept his mouth shut. He didn't want to speak ever again, amid all this deception hanging thick in the air. His head felt as though it had been submerged in lava.

Nevertheless, he managed to fall asleep. He dreamed of men with golden eyes, wearing black clothes, roaming a landscape of small black hills with yellow gashes studded with ancient brown bones, where flying reptiles with wings on their arms and legs swooped down on their prey. He wandered through this landscape until he came upon several of the reptiles feeding on a boy's carcass.

The boy was him.

Vlad woke up with a scream. He switched on the bedside lamp and went to the kitchen in his bare feet to get a glass of orange juice. He drank thirstily. The kitchen windows showed bright lights, traffic, high buildings, and a neat pattern of streets. The glass clinked loudly when he put it down. He'd now cracked it by accident.

Eventually, he went back to bed, knowing that his attempts to sleep would most likely be fruitless. The lights of the strange land shone outside his window, through the drizzle-speckled glass. He soon entered a strange state of mind somewhere between consciousness and unconsciousness.

Two weeks later, his parents welcomed him into a gabled townhouse with black shingles and grey bricks—a rather Gothic look, it seemed to him, one that matched the grey sky that morning. He was amazed at the size of the townhouse, which stood in sharp contrast with the apartment back in Moscow. Was this a castle? Had morguds built it? His parents couldn't hide from him the fact that Toronto was Layer One, Layer One Toronto.

Then he started Grade 8. The other students began to look like morguds, with black clothes and golden bright eyes. He lashed out at one boy during recess. The boy had said something or other, and Vlad had jumped upon him, thrown him onto the ground, and pummelled him repeatedly while screaming, "I know you're all morguds!"

His parents were called to the school. When they got back, his father asked, "What's going on, son?"

"I know they're all morguds, Dad," Vlad said. Finally, he'd said it! He'd exposed the lie.

"I think something's wrong with him," his father said.

"Just a teenage thing," his mother disagreed.

"We must find someone from Layer One," his father said, suddenly looking much older than his age. Vlad considered running away in the night with a backpack filled with some supplies. The morguds would never get him!

That weekend—he didn't run away, couldn't figure out where he'd go—his father forcibly drove him to the access point from which they'd emerged, the kind of place that had supplanted the airports of old, allegedly more efficient as well as better for the environment, although his father expressed bitter reservations as he drove. As usual, he waved his hands, letting go of the wheel frequently, while he made his declamations. "Those fools say it's safe! Son, you've gone mad. You don't know what you're saying anymore. That place made you crazy!"

Vlad viewed his father with suspicion. What the hell was that old man going on about?

"I'm going to make them fix this," his father went on. He was rambling like a maniac.

Father and son pulled up at the brick building flaunting a row of white columns in front of the main entrance, like a museum. This made it seem as though they would soon meet something mightier than a morgud, perhaps something that really controlled this circus show from behind the scenes. "We'll make him talk, whether he wants to or not," his father said as he walked rapidly. Vlad could just keep up, although he constantly looked around, wondering whether he could dash for the exit and escape this vast conspiracy. He knew they were still in that dark in-between land!

They barged into the room where the access point for Moscow was housed. His father made his way past the line, eliciting shouts of fury and disbelief, until he reached the man with golden eyes. "My son has gone mad. After going through your Layer. He's gone off the deep end! And gets into violent fights at school! He gave that other boy a hellish thrashing, and for what?"

The morgud considered him for a moment. "What am I supposed to do about it?"

"He's been talking crazy nonsense and not acting like himself. He's fighting kids at school. He's going nuts, and it's your fault! Your stupid 'safe' mode of travel!"

The man looked at the angry Russian before him and the angry people in line. His eyes flicked back and forth a few times. Then he sighed. "Follow me." Disregarding the people's protests, the morgud led the father and son duo onto the disc. It lit up with a bright white light. It turned out that multiple people could go through at the same time, at least when accompanied by a morgud. "I think the transition was too stressful for him. And he has a weak mind. There are noxious elements in the air that can drive a weak mind insane."

"You will cure him."

"I can't," the man said. "But I know someone who can help."

Just as his father reached out to grab the man and shake him, the morgud turned his back on them and walked rapidly toward the hills. "Follow me," he said quickly over his shoulder.

They walked for quite some time. Finally, they reached a wooden house on top of one of the hills. Wooden steps led up to the house. The man with golden eyes ascended and knocked on the door. Vlad knew that they wanted to kill him, knew it in every fibre of his being. That's why they'd brought him here, to kill him, because he knew too much and could see past the scam.

"Come in," a frail but mischievous-sounding voice responded.

The three went in. Vlad stood in the door, ready to run away at the first sign of their murderous attempts to subdue him. An old man sat on a cot, surrounded by dusty books.

"The kid has lost it," the man with golden eyes said. "Looks like a case of extreme disorientation. Could be a side effect of the journey."

"I see," the old man said. Then he coughed into his fist. It was a prolonged coughing fit. Then he ran his finger along a shelf full of vials filled with liquids all colours of the rainbow.

"Who are you?" Vlad asked. His voice shook with rage. "Why did you bring me here?"

"I'm an alchemist and a healer," the old man answered without looking around. Then he said, "Aha," and took down a vial filled with a green liquid with silver bubbles. "Drink this," he said.

"What is this?" Vlad's father asked.

"Never mind. He must drink it."

The old man removed the cork. Vlad started running away, but his father grabbed him, helped by the morgud. They were going to kill him! He wriggled and thrashed in their grasp. They were killing him! The old man poured the concoction down his throat. Immediately, Vlad fell onto the floor, convulsing, only the whites of his eyes showing.

"Oh, crap, I gave him the wrong one." The old man scanned the shelf again, just as Vlad's father reached for him with murderous hands. "There, that's it! A lighter shade of green. Make him drink it."

While Vlad was slowly departing from this world, from every world, his father lifted his head off the floor and allowed the new liquid to trickle between his lips. The convulsions slowed, and Vlad gradually regained his full awareness. He looked at the remaining liquid in the vial.

"You have to keep drinking this," the old man said. "You'll have to come back to me every day. It'll work if you give it enough time to work."

The morgud led them back to the access point, even though Vlad's father screamed about the error that had been made and the seeming death sentence, having to visit Layer One with such constancy and frequency and for such an extreme length of time. By now, the crowd was going berserk. Father and son hurried to the car to avoid getting killed. Then they drove back to the little town. Toronto? A morgud conspiracy? Of course, it was a morgud conspiracy. They'd poisoned him.

Vlad went to his room and shut the door. He sat there for a long time, listening to their shouting match downstairs. They were arguing about him and what had happened in Layer One.

"If he doesn't take it, by God, I'll stuff it down his throat!" his father screamed.

They would keep poisoning him, robbing him of his knowledge that there was a morgud conspiracy. He slept fitfully that night, not knowing his future. Everything felt surrounded by a grey fog. He was on shaky ground, but his parents sounded determined to keep feeding him the supposedly healing potion. He felt resigned to that, not wanting to live on the street. He would hide his secret knowledge from them, about the morgud stuff. They'd locked him into a prison, but he knew the truth.

ABOUT THE AUTHOR

Paul Lebedev

Previous contributor to an IWA anthology

Paul Lebedev was born in Moscow and grew up in southern Ontario. He works as a copywriter and holds a Bachelor of Arts in English from the University of Toronto.

With a vivid imagination nurtured by nature walks, Paul is passionate about fiction writing.

Several of his short stories and one poem were published in *Voices* 2016–2020 and in three IWA anthologies.

Paul is the author of *Portals* (a collection of short stories), the novel *Chosen by Nature*, the upcoming novel *Into the Forest*, and other books.

Connect with Paul Lebedev:

- Amazon.com/author/paullebedev
- Facebook page: Paul.lebedev.author

BREAKING FREE

BY MARNI DIEANU

Every so often we sit with ourselves in a pattern of mistakes, our mistakes, because we can't blame anybody for the steps we've taken as adults. But what if these patterns are nothing else than pieces of a puzzle that we put together following the same cultural pattern that has been ingrained in our veins for generations?

We carry with us our individual traumas; we carry with us the collective trauma of our nations, but how about the societal ideas?

We all get tangled in humanity's collective rules, beliefs, and practices about life in general—what education, career, love life, happiness, financial standing, and health is considered more successful. Add to this the cultural differences between one country and another, the historical torments, and the individual is caught up in a web.

But how does one person break free? How do you move from always bending to life's necessities and blindly accepting preconceived rules, to being yourself and finding your own way?

This is HER story, that of an immigrant woman, a daughter, a wife, a mother, an employee, a friend trying to find her way without having a label on her forehead as to what she should be.

Her diary

March 15, 2020

Thanks, God, for the Internet ... in these times when we are all to stay isolated, we are still connected. Stay safe everyone!

April 2, 2020

I want out! Out of this apartment, out of this life, out of everything.

There are so many things mixing in my head right now. I slept three and a half hours last night, so I can't think straight. Since self-isolation on March 16 … I sleep four to six hours. After a month like this, I bet my brain is not functioning properly.

July 2, 2020

I'm doing what I can to keep my spirits up. And seriously, it's not really working. One moment I am beside myself with hope, the next I drown in despair. All those self-improvement books and videos just help me stay afloat. This pandemic put even more pressure and stress on me. I sleep very little, and I can't focus. The children are at home; my husband's job has closed; my job may close, and that adds to the pressure …

. . .

About two weeks ago, I had a big crisis—a sleepless night and racing thoughts, and I just crashed. Instead of leaving me alone to calm down, my husband called my mom, and that's when I exploded, like a bomb. I kept my children near me—it calms me down. I said some harsh things. When we are angry, we all say a lot of things that we regret later. But I felt terrible about the way I acted towards my children, like I'm such an inappropriate mom. They offer me so much unconditional love and although things are challenging, children are always sweet. And I failed them. I feel we are all losing it …

December 14, 2020

Calling it a rollercoaster sounds nice. I don't have much time because of work and stuff, BUT I have to put this down. Today, I am looking at an online art magazine where a painting of mine has been shared as an example of pandemic art. I cried a lot. I may never be a famous artist; I don't know if any of my paintings will ever sell, but this is such an accomplishment for me, a life dream, my painting not just hanging on the school's walls.

December 25, 2020

This year has been messed up, and I have been trying super hard. Sleeping just four, five hours per night didn't help. I forget when I last washed my hair, maybe three weeks ago. We've put all our major payments on hold. The pressure of it all crushed me slowly, and I started experiencing health problems. In the summer, I ended up in ER. I've been blaming myself; I've been blaming him, everybody. I felt suffocated and trapped, as if drowning. I felt so frustrated because I wasn't performing at maximum capacity with anything:

- Work required me more and more because of the pandemic. No one respected the working hours anymore (not that I usually had a regular schedule). Plus, there is always the pressure of proving that you are doing a great job even when working from home.
- The house felt a perpetual mess because we were all at home.
- The kids complained that I didn't spend time with them. Who had this great idea that a parent can monitor children of different ages online and offline while working a full-time job and taking care of the house?
- I found out I have an incurable illness.

Every second I feel like a pot of boiling water. Is this the life I signed up for? And yet, this was the year I promised myself I would do better. We've been fighting so much, I divorced him in my head a billion times. And if I hear one more person saying to take this time to learn something new, I swear I'm going to punch him or her in the face. It was lucky that we were all mandated into isolation.

I'm glad I started painting again, at midnight when I was in pain and couldn't sleep. My biggest achievement was my shared painting, also it was the only one.

When I heard he got a job, I cried. I felt so happy and relieved for us. I wish he were as happy for me.

Author's notes: January 2021–June 2021

There are no records for this period, but according to sources, this is what happened:

• She lost her best friend to COVID-19.

• She lost her grandma to COVID-19.

• She couldn't attend any of the funerals.

• Her parents got COVID-19 and were alone without help for a couple of weeks, in a faraway country with a questionable medical system.

• Her health deteriorated, and she required more medical assistance.

• She had two suicide attempts.

• She lost her job.

• She consulted a lawyer to sue her employer for misconduct and abandoned the effort because she was too weak for a legal process.

Her diary:

June 5, 2021

I'm sitting here in the park with a cup of steaming coffee—because only I could enjoy hot coffee in the depth of summer trying to figure out things, to put my life in order, and truth be told, I have no idea where to start. I realized that over the years I missed out on so many things just because I put others first, just because I simply tried to survive. I think it's about time I put myself first. My self-sabotaging mind is still trying to find excuses, but wouldn't this be better than living a life full of regrets and unhappiness?

June 6, 2021

Can I just be during this time? Can I just be alive with no other expectations? I'm so tired mentally and physically, and I just want to lie down and never wake up, just like that, so no one has to deal with the ugly part that I took my own life. And then my children pop into my head, and I wonder how I can be better for them when I can't even find a way to live. How do I survive?

July 5, 2021

I know how I feel—tired mentally and physically. I write a phrase every few minutes—it's as if my brain is frozen. Can you imagine how tired I am? How many years of tiredness I bring with me? How do you start living and start smiling again? How do you reprogram your entire brain?

August 12, 2021

Last night I took a picture of my living room at 10 pm. One can only imagine my frustration. Every toy on that carpet has its place in my children's story, and I was not allowed to touch it because today they were going to play again.

I wanted to post it, wondering if other parents go through this, but somehow, I got caught up in other things and my desperate need for a moment of peace.

Sometimes, I wonder how other parents' houses look during this pandemic with kids continuously at home. Everyone is always trying to share their perfect self, a perfect moment, beautiful things—how about the messes? Don't we all mess up?

This morning as I was talking with a group of moms, we all realized that sometimes you just have to let it go and not stress over everything. They are kids just once ... and our need for perfection and cleanliness may not always match with our children's beautiful play mess.

October 30, 2021

Today, I was sharpening a pencil, and a memory related to my former job came to me. I had a pencil at work that I sharpened every time I was angry about something. I held inside me the fury about the things I thought unfair and told myself that one day—when there will be nothing left of that pencil, I'll find the courage to move on.

When I first came to Canada, I promised myself that I would be open to starting everything from zero, schooling, work, everything. I had so much hope and confidence in myself. However, not everything went according to plan.

First of all, I didn't expect racism. I didn't expect people to say to your face that they are not giving you the job, not because you don't know the language, but because you are not from here, you have a European accent. I didn't expect that an education and a professional background really counted for nothing here, regardless where in the world they were obtained. I didn't expect that people would try to trick you, including immigrants who may have gone through the same hardships.

And, then, it didn't go according to plan, because I didn't know any better or because I was ill advised. If I had known then what I know now ... I would have fought harder for my rights and my dreams.

No matter how much you read and inform yourself before moving to a new country, there would still be things that an immigrant hasn't foreseen.

And one has to survive.

I set my dreams aside, and I found security. I gained over the years what some would consider the perfect life: a beautiful family, a job, and nice place I called home. Isn't that how everybody from outside sees an immigrant's life?

During the pandemic, I got burned out. Working from home in a demanding job with kids that needed attention became unbearable. I couldn't even clean up without someone making a mess behind my back. Plus, it was always looming over us, the possibility of losing the job. "Lucky enough to still have a job!" as someone put it. I was stuck.

By the summer of 2021, I was suffocating. I was sick physically and utterly exhausted.

I needed a break ... I knew then that I had to do something to change my life completely.

My partner and everyone else close to me suggested changing jobs.

Why do we do jobs that burn us out, jobs we come to hate? Because we need money to survive. It's sad because I actually loved my job at one point.

However, I dread having to work again in that field. The mere thought puts a claw around my neck; it burns and I stop breathing, I want to be me! And as I fiddled trying to find myself and applying randomly for jobs in other similar fields, at one point I understood I had to take a leap of faith.

I felt I was like a goat jumping from one peak to another, ignoring the void below. Everybody was telling me to stick to the pattern ... eat the grass they all eat—find that job, get security. As an immigrant you can't afford the luxury of trying things.

Because that's what first-generation immigrants stick to— security ... they work in jobs that they don't like or that burn them out. Poorly paid, they work hard to prove themselves, to keep a roof over their heads and to put food in their bellies because there is no option to go back, and they need to secure a future for the next generation.

"There are thousands waiting at the door for your job," as my employer once said to me. The sacrificing generation ...

November 2, 2021

And maybe one day I'll break the pattern, open a door, and be vulnerable in the eyes of the world—with a strong feeling, paving a path for other souls, as wild and handcuffed as I've ever felt.

That's how I felt all my life, like a bird in a cage, with wings, but captive.

Any struggle hurt its wings; it was unable to get free.

And one day, the bird realized that there is no longer a heavy padlock on the door, that it could come out, that the door has been without a padlock for a long time, although closed. She could have come out, but she didn't come out.

Do you know why it didn't come out? Because it got used to the cage, where for good or for bad she could sleep, she received water and food, and all she did, was—sing. In fact, she sang poorly, because her voice had lost its vigour. She sang because that was her purpose, but her song was blunted. She could have pushed open the door and flown, but she didn't fly because she didn't know anything about the outside world, because she didn't know if her wings were still working, because she didn't know if she could still fly, because she was afraid. The comfort ...

Even in a prison, it's nice for someone who expects nothing but misery, cold, hunger, and violence outside. Clothes, food, and a bed away from the rain. Such basics are attractive to someone who has nothing.

What if I can still fly?

November 4, 2021

My mind is a mixture of languages depending on the moment—now I think in French, in two hours in English. I dream in Italian, and then I am romantic in Spanish. German seems as complicated as my soul. And heavy. I tried to learn it, but it didn't stick. I need a simple, harmonious language ...

I don't even know what I wanted to write any more ... I was confused by the book waiting to be finished, I still have two pages, but I was hungry.

Ah, today ...

I squealed like a child when he asked me:

"Did you see what I got you?"

I've put together the whole shopping list. I knew very well what he had.

"Quince," I finally replied. "But I can't eat today," I added quickly. "I am sick."

I dream of quince. I cut them and feel their taste ...

Tomorrow, maybe tomorrow I can eat.

I also thought about boiling them since I saw them—just to eat.

But I made myself a soup—the worst soup ever—I cut two potatoes in four, a handful of whole carrots, and a half onion, salt and parsley at the end.

I gave him stew, and I brought the cheese and spices to the table ... these are not missing from any table in our other country.

The children have not touched the stew. They don't eat mixtures.

I'll never cook again, I tell myself. It looked so good when I did it. I couldn't believe it.

The soup is ok, it's tasty, but in an hour, I'll hear it bubbling in my stomach. At least I don't throw up. And let me not start coughing or wheezing again when I go out grocery shopping. In these Covidian times, hearing someone cough is the worst —it doesn't matter if it's not COVID-19; the looks, the distance, the get-out signs.

Some days are so soft ... I do what I can, I tell myself. I can barely stand.

I had plans for today—I bought so many canvases and paints.

I ought to call the doctor, but I don't seem to have the strength to do that either. Plus, I don't even feel like calling when I think how I'm going to be treated. Why are some doctors so indifferent to people's suffering? Will one treat me better than the other?

I will lie down—I'm dizzy and tired.

I have five minutes left, and I have to leave ...

Sometimes we just need to stay ... a little, a day, an eternity.

I have given up so much in everything I have done. I have sacrificed so much for my jobs, for my studies, for my family, and I seem to have lost all my energy. Now I feel the need to sit ... to gather, to recover ... and time passes and nothing is enough ...

I need myself ... a little more.

November 8, 2021

I started to think that having a full night's sleep is the stuff of legend. May my coffee be strong, my day short and my focus high.

There are days when you wonder what went wrong. Days like this, when you ask yourself why you can't fight. When did you lose your energy? Why are you always so drained? Why?

November 11, 2021

Hope

I stay a little with today, with yesterday, with tomorrow, with me, with you, with us. I've been staying a while.

I painted yesterday. It was beautiful, liberating. But weak. I feel like screaming at myself. But I shut up, I drive away such thoughts. How far I would have come now if my father had let me do art. But art doesn't pay the bills. His words still resonate in my mind: "And what are you going to be, a starving artist?"

I have talent, but it's unworked. If I were an art teacher, maybe I would be happier than doing a job that I forced myself to love. Back then, in that country, one had to choose a field that brought money. I should have changed that when I came to Canada, but I continued on the same path. I got so caught up in this game, hoping that it would make me happy.

We need money to survive ... all right, we survived and got nowhere. Because people take advantage of others, they burn you out for their own good, disregarding your needs. Somewhere in the middle of the road I stopped because I couldn't go any further, because I wasn't there anymore. For about eight years I fought with who I am. I don't know how I got stuck even harder. It was like walking through mud. Good thing my first child came. Like a white bird that landed on my shoulder when I was still struggling in the mud. And I swear I didn't really know what to do ... I soiled my children with my muddy hands. Seriously now, kids don't come with textbooks. And even if they did, the problem is not them; it is us and our baggage of hollow stories that have weakened our souls. A new parent who has his hands hidden, his body marked by scars, and voices in his head does not know how to catch a baby without causing an injury to the child.

But honestly, without my white pigeons I don't think I would have gotten out of the mud ... because we all need a miracle, rainbow children, to light our way and make us better, someone or something that will motivate us to get out of the mud, to move on and not give up the fight. I knelt down many times, and I thought I was going to die there with my head down, suffocated in misery when I heard the baby cry. They stopped me so many times from going crazy, even when they were having a fit.

I don't know what to expect next. But I still hope that I will make enough money to live and offer them what I didn't have. I hope.

November 28, 2021

I felt free for a while, and when you feel happy, you live. But yesterday I broke again.

You know what is the worst thing someone can say to you? That your passion is just a hobby. And that's what my family has been telling me my whole life.

It feels as if every time I feel I could fly, I fell again. I didn't know that breaking free also takes time.

December 31, 2021

I lost people this year to COVID-19, and most importantly, I learned to appreciate the simple act of being alive.

It has not been easy to acknowledge those situations that are out of our reach, but I know I stood up for the ones I could still fight. Because for sure no one is coming to save you except yourself.

I've seen myself at my worst, but also at my best.

In the first half of the year, I hit rock bottom, and in the other half, I tried to pick up the pieces of myself, like those of a puzzle, and put them back together or simply create something new.

Maybe I didn't achieve anything major this year, and yet a few moments made me feel perfect. And it's those moments when I felt most alive that I want to keep and nurture.

Goodbye 2021. I am not sure how 2022 will be, and for sure there will be moments we can't control, but for the others, I wish for us all to keep on watering our own garden.

May flowers sprout from the seeds we keep on planting. May we find beauty in the simple things, and may we all stay healthy. I wish for myself to keep on growing and be myself.

Happy New Year!

. . .

January, 2022

I stay there on top of the fence, like a hawk waiting for my prey. Only there is no prey, it's just me on the fence. I wish I could explain this feeling that paralyzes my veins. I wish I could explain the invisible heavy chains that hold me down. It is not easy to break free when all your life you've been dragging those chains around.

February, 2022

War started … yes, because this is exactly what the world needs after two pandemic years. I bawl my eyes out following the news. Some of the comments sound like—there has always been war, hunger and a bunch of problems going around—like increased food and gas prices; real-estate market out of control; since 2020, all sorts of COVID-19 related restrictions; high unemployment rates; and for us Canadians, cold winters.

I carry with me the pain of my ancestors—refugees from past wars and immigrants looking for a better life who always reinvented themselves in a new environment. Maybe that's why I relate so much to this story of war:

My great-grandfather was a six-year-old orphan crossing a thousand kilometres on foot, running from a different Russian invasion. He was adopted by a family that treated him as a slave. My other ancestors from the other side of the family were also refugees, from a Turk invasion. My other great-grandfather immigrated to a new country for a better life, only to be dragged into a war that destroyed everything he had built. Our grandparents lost everything and ended up in communist prisons. Persecuted. Always restarting from zero.

"My dream as a child was to be able to eat a banana every day," my husband said to me once.

"Mine too," I said, hugging him.

We've come such a long way. I know this as I glance at the darkened banana that soon will be transformed into banana bread, just so we don't waste anything. Ancestral trauma runs in our blood.

Why should I bother with someone else's war? But focusing on someone else's war distracts me from the war inside my head and from the physical pain. My pain sounds unreasonable.

They've been telling me to get a job in my field. But I've also been told:

"What in the world do you think you are doing?"

"You can't even hold a job!"

"You are the worst mom ever!"

"You are a disappointment as a daughter."

"Do you think you are the only one who worked hard?"

"Do you think you are the only one who broke down?"

"Do you think you are the only one who was cheated on?"

"Housework is not work."

"You are an entitled bitch!"

"You never finish anything."

"You are always sick."

"You are too old."

"You are too late."

"Miss Piggy. Pork Chop. You can't even work out."

"If you don't like Canadian winters, go back home."

"You are always in bed, watching TV."

"Who do you think you are?"

"You are a nobody."

"You are a failure."

"It's all in your head."

"You won't amount to anything."

"You wanted equality?"

"Get a hold of yourself; this is how life is."

"Stop bitching about this and that. Suck it up!"

You … you … you are not enough! But I am enough! I want to scream! I'm doing the best I can—isn't that enough? I've always given my all.

Burnout doesn't exist and mental health is something shameful. If you have a physical problem, you toughen up and keep on moving.

"Do you think I don't want to stay home and peel potatoes and play with my kids?" I heard a friend say to his wife when we were all discussing housework division. "But I have to work outside the house."

It may be a cultural thing.

. . .

March 4, 2022

Unheard of in my culture—taking a break, to breathe and heal.

March 23, 2022

Fear is paralyzing, but I will not let fear define me. As I write this, I feel as if my feet are in a cold stream.

Failure! The word was blared at me in different forms every time I opened my mouth about a new idea on what to do next.

While at the beginning, I was saying confidently that "I believe in myself," soon my mind was filled with dread. I was paralyzed. I couldn't paint anymore or continue the therapy program—I had a hard time starting or finishing anything because all I could see was the void. The "good advice of others" was not positive for my mind.

And one day it dawned on me: "Does the goat know there is a void? Does she acknowledge it as I do? Or does she jump blindly?"

What if I jump blindly? I might fall and die, if I were a goat, or I could be on the peak I wanted to be on. Every morning, when a new day starts, I try to tell myself "But what if you could fly?"

Yes, the void is still there, but I decided to focus on my destination.

It is slow and hard and most days, I felt I wasn't making any progress—there was always something that interrupted my plans—my health, chores, the children. I had days when I felt it was best if I had a stable job, because then there was a somehow secure income at the end of the month.

But what I didn't understand then was that even on those days when I was struggling to get anything done, I was becoming stronger, I was embracing my real me.

I was reading Gabriela's journey from the IWA anthology *Moving Forward*—and the idea of jumping into the void stayed with me. I didn't even finish reading when I decided it was time to write my own story. So, I stayed up that night until dawn and wrote my story.

On top of these things, it was one of the days when I was bedridden and completely exhausted after a month in which every member of my family had been sick. We were bound to get COVID-19 at some point, right? And when you are an immigrant and you have no one to help you, you know that you can't afford to be sick ... someone has to cook, do the laundry, feed the kids, and ideally also make some money. My partner and I take turns like sentinels in the night.

But my story has to be written!

Typically, people build their self-confidence on things that are constantly changing. It's like the story of the builders who constructed their gorgeous house on sand. We continuously allow the things around us to define our confidence. In order to have personal confidence, one needs to know the rules of the game. But what are the rules of the game? There are none in the game of how to live your own life.

We struggle to stay afloat and smile for a pretty picture just to appear as if we're loving life when in reality there's nothing easy about it, there are clouds above, and huge waves, and the water is cold in the middle of summer, because it's Canada.

So, I'm dropping the act! I am allowed to be broken. I am allowed to take time to heal! I am allowed to reinvent myself.

I won't let my culture define who I am supposed to be! I am free! I am me! Only I can grasp what I've been through. Only I can figure out who I am supposed to be! This is my legacy!

I am breaking free!

—

Author's Note:

For this story, I kept alive the discussions and messages I exchanged with many other women during the pandemic.

I started it from my own Facebook posts, but it slowly became everybody else's story.

I wanted women to feel heard. You are not alone! We are all continuously finding our own way.

ABOUT THE AUTHOR

Marni Dieanu

Previous contributor to an IWA anthology

Marni Dieanu is a first-generation Canadian immigrant. She lived in several places around the world before making Toronto her home.

Marni has published works in English, Romanian, and French. She is contributing for the third time to the IWA anthology with another story on human resilience and immigrant strength in adjusting to a new environment.

With two Master's degrees in Communications and PR, Marni wrote for business most of her adult life. However, she never forgot her love for literature (fiction and poetry).

Marni is passionate about artistic expression in words, visual arts, or dance.

Connect with Marni Dieanu:

- Marnidieanu.com
- Instagram: @serenia.art

FROM WHERE I ONCE STOOD

BY KIMBERLY J. KIRT

TRUE NORTH

They say it's easier to live in a Border City
If you must leave your country, better to plant
One foot on each side

LIMBO.

"You're closer to Home than those who cross oceans,"
they say.
"It'll be a smoother ride."

And while Home is just a 13-hour drive,
Coasting down a rolling freeway
in the middle of the night
If I could afford it, a one-hour plane ride

But it's been a year
And I still don't have a job that pays my bills
Much less the immigration fees
Both Over and Under qualified

Seven years of University schooling
And two US degrees

"But surely it must be easier being American,
the culture is mostly the same"

While I'm standing in line at a local Tim Hortons,
wondering what it means to order a *Double-Double*
Two tables over,
a group laughs out loud
"Those fucking Americans—
no wonder they're so fat,"
a man says
As he shoves a donut down

Another replies and nods his head,
"Gun-happy hillbillies they all are"
Nearby tables cluck in agreement

The teenagers in line behind me roar with laughter
My body tightens and I stay silent
Remembering the US/Canada pin I proudly placed
on the backpack I always wear
For my job-searching days at the library

I ask the cashier for an Iced Capp
It's the only item I know
Because back Home, I used to like Caramel Coolers

And I think that's sort of the same thing.

"But it's much easier living on a Border City—
you're just a river-cross away"

I must admit,

in the first two years it was nice
To be able to catch a weak signal
on my US cellphone
From the banks of the Detroit River

Gazing across at a strange US city—
The only connection to Home in sight
Asking my family and friends on the other line
With tears spilling from my eyes,

"When is it going to get easier,
this new life of mine?"

I came to Canada for Love,
Hoping it would be more
Embraced
Proving the "validity" of my Love
on an IMM-5532 form[1]
Was only a taste of sealed Fate

"It must be so much easier
Loving a woman in Canada
than it was in the US"

I've been told to hide and deny
the depths of my soul
to stop holding hands
and displaying love notes
Told my Love was unacceptable,
cat-calls and undertones
treated as a phase or some joke

More than I ever was back Home.

Immigration has taught me

That Hatred exists everywhere

But
so does
Love.

[So does Love]

It has been nearly a decade now
and I still wonder
If I'll ever truly settle with where I've been

But I've worked hard to build
a semblance of the life
I'd left behind

Finding my way
Against all odds in the dark,

An Invisible Immigrant's Compass
Still points to the Heart.

DIVERGENT

I exist
As two different people
Two identities crossed
Split between
Life Before
and
Life After
Feeling a Traitor
Though I've never felt more loyal

To my countries
Waving flags of both in each hand,
The one that built me
And the one I chose

Lost

On the path to where I've been

Seeking the way
That leads me Home.

HIRAETH[2]

My Bridge to Somewhere
Seems like a lifetime
Since I've seen you
in the light that I used to
Connecting both my worlds
So close
Too far
With the safety of an exit
Couldn't see where I was headed
For now,
Just trying to get to where I'm going
Whether there are other bridges
To somewhere
Waiting for me
To cross
Or burn
Makes no difference.

I'd swim to the place that felt like

Home
if I had to.

CAN-AM

They crossed oceans
Like I crossed freeways
The lady behind the desk at
Settlement Services
Says that's not the same thing

But I know better.

Thirteen Hours
by Plane or Car
Still rewinds and stalls Time
The cost of starting over
A clean slate,
Is all the money you've ever
Made
Along with everything you've ever
Built
Stacked tightly beside all you've ever
Been, or wanted to be
The flag patched onto the back of
Your rolling suitcase
And the dizzying miles in-between
The Past and Future
Makes no difference
How far you've come
To get to where you're going
Home shrinking until it disappears
In windows
And in mirrors

They will never understand the price paid
To finally get to a place
That seems to have never wanted you.

CONSTRUCTION

In the time that surrounds
These years
There is one bridge I haven't burned
Some of the hardest things to long for
Are the bridges you can cross
But won't.

And I have contemplated
The distance between
The sound of each wave
Crashing
Into worn fences
Paint chipped, carved memories
Names and dates strung across
Displayed promises
Broken or kept.

A hovering road above
Could take me anywhere but here
And I'm always reaching backwards
So close, yet so far
From knowing what matters.

But there is a flag that rests
Behind me
Glorified stars and stripes
There are flags everywhere
And I think it's time

To find mine.

IF IT'S SO EASY TO CROSS, WHY DON'T YOU

Do you feel the imaginary lines
That make your borders now?

Now that you're stuck in time
Forced to pick sides
Which Home will you choose
Before the gates close
On the life you once knew
Can't reach your Friends

Well, I felt that for years
Pulling signals from parked cars
Watching houses get smaller
In rearview mirrors
And I'd commit myself to a place
That set fire to my dreams
They had nothing good to say of me
Of my roots
My culture
My needs
So many of us have fallen silent
Forgotten who we were
Trying to cross your Invisible
Impossible
Boundaries
Are you feeling the pressure now?
Do you feel the tension now?
All the sacrifices we've made

Trying to find Home.

REARVIEW MIRRORS

I cross daily in my mind
A silent plea between space and time
Connecting all the love that I've known

Only roads separate
My Heart
and my Home

TO SPLIT YOUR HEART IN TWO

They don't ask me what I miss
But they say I must be used to the snow
How right they are
So used to what I'm used to
Makes loving this city hard

FROM WHERE I ONCE STOOD

Home is in
those 9 pm planes
Lighting up my skyline
Reminding me
of the life I left behind

Home is not that far away

Just one bridge to cross
And a thirteen-hour drive
I could be there tonight.
But highways are lonely

And maybe Home has become
A place where I would feel
lonelier than I do here
That Critical Point
Between what was
And what is
Am I finally seeing the difference?
I still count the years
But I no longer count the stars
City-filtered light
Can you still see them
from where you are?

7EVEN

It's been seven years now
The road Home has merged
Into what feels like a two-way street
A space in time still exists
where they both meet

If life's all about choices,
Then I put all my chips in
Traded Familiarity for Fate
And black coffee for Double-Doubles
And patterned stars of glimmering past
for blinding city lights

Not all choices are so easy
A rope around my heart
Tugs gently, ever-present
Love is Heavy
but so Alive

They say that every seven years
You're given new skin
I've grown into
The places I've been
Traveled so far
From the person I've been

Over the years
I've built a bridge to connect my Home
And my Heart,
Forever existing in both.
Through every tide
And place and time,
The Faith to carry me—

Where I'm meant to be.

IMM-T60025****[3]

In my dream last night
You asked me if I wanted to come home
I said I want to
But I can't
You said, "I understand."
The ruby slippers I wear
To get me there
I keep kicking off my feet

There is no in-between
When your heart believes.
I hate when people ask me
How I like it here
I never know what to say
Is it too honest to say
I traded in my Home
And people who loved me
For a little amount of Faith
A small price to pay
For the One I love.
But seven years in
And I still can't answer
What I love about this place
Besides Her
A pin on a map
Where I don't belong
I've drowned myself in more tears
Here
Than anywhere I've ever been.

They say it shouldn't be any different
But I'm still counting the weeks and days
They say it should be no different
than the Home I came from [As they laugh at my Stars and
Stripes]

THE SUN SETS IN BOTH MY COUNTRIES

I've learned to love this city with
Resistance
Perseverance
Forgiveness

And now I don't care if it loves me back
The sunsets are so beautiful
And with each sunrise
I become
more Alive.

TO MAKE A HEART A HOME

It took me a long time to love this city.

But I fell in love here.
I have done the most growing here.
Built some of my biggest dreams here.
Cried the most tears here.
Learned the most lessons here.

It took a long time.

But this city has become a place I hold in the spaces of my heart, alongside other places I've called Home.

Now I don't know where I belong, if belonging is a place.
But I will follow my Heart to the edge of the world, toward what matters most.

Fight for what's most important to you.

This city [and this country] taught me that.

———

1
Canada's Relationship and Sponsorship Application Immigration form that assesses the relationship between spouses and common-law partners.

2
Welsh pronunciation: [hɪraɨθ, hiːraɨθ]. A Welsh word that has no direct English translation. Nostalgia, yearning, homesickness, a longing to be where your spirit lives.

3
Case ID Number assigned to Permanent Residence applicants from initiation of the immigration process until final approval of Permanent Residency.

ABOUT THE AUTHOR

Kimberly J. Kirt

Kimberly J. Kirt is originally from Minnesota in the United States. She moved to Canada for Love in 2012, and completed the immigration process for her Permanent Residence in 2013. The year of this book release is special, as it marks her decade year of living in Canada.

Kimberly holds a Bachelor's degree in Creative Writing and a Master's degree in Community Counselling from the United States.

Kimberly wants to use her experiences and lessons learned to shine a light for others who may be struggling to "find their way." She believes that Hope is a powerful navigation tool.

Connect with Kimberly J. Kirt:

- Linkedin.com/in/kimberly-j-k

LIFE SHOWED ME THE WAY

BY GABRIELA CASINEANU

We must let go of the life we have planned
to accept the one that is waiting for us.
~ Joseph Campbell

One day, I found this message for Introverts Academy: "I'm an extrovert! I am a people person. I have a problem with intros. Very bad experience."

"What problem?" I was curious.

"A relative. She is an intro. When I say hi to her, she never replies."

There could be many reasons the person to whom she refers behaved that way. Some might not even relate to introversion. Anyway, I mentioned that introverts are also *people persons* and added a link to a video about the complementary innate traits of introverts and extroverts.

Her "thank you" ended the conversation.

This discussion stayed with me for a while. It reminded me, once again, why it was a good idea to build the Introverts Academy. However, I never thought of starting this project before 2020, when life gave me a sign … as it did many times before.

Throughout the years, I came to believe that life already has a path lined up for me. And it keeps showing signs and taking me through unexpected experiences (which totally makes sense after a while) that are building blocks to pave that path.

My latest project, for example, the Introverts Academy. A platform that offers resources, online courses, videos, books, coaching, and training to raise awareness about the introverts' strengths—and how to tap into their impressive inner power for personal, professional, organizational, and systemic development—to build a better world for all of us.

The insight to start the Introverts Academy hit me in December 2020. In the previous two months, I focused on another project that didn't seem to be sustainable long term. Tired both physically and mentally, I took a break between Christmas and the New Year to do … nothing. Just relax and stay open to catching any signs life could throw on me.

It didn't take long! The fourth day, a sudden thought caught my attention: "Build an Introverts Academy!"

I laughed. How come I didn't think of this before?

After all, life helped me build so many skills and useful expertise for this meaningful project. Many of which were triggered by unexpected situations. It also gave me clear signs that doing something related to *introversion* is part of my life's purpose.

The Engineering Years

My professional career started in electronics engineering, although that was not my first choice.

In school, I became good at math and physics because my mom taught me logical thinking at a younger age. Loving maths, she was eager to pass it on to her youngest daughter— who would rather play outside with friends, dance, sing, or draw landscapes with palms on a beach. Well, my mom succeeded.

My father didn't allow me to register at a high school specialized in IT, a field that attracted me because of its creative side. "You need to enhance your general knowledge, not specialize in something from such a young age," he said while registering me at one of the best high schools in Brasov (Romania). During the last year, I thought of becoming an architect (the design part appealed to me), but my mom was afraid that I wouldn't pass the technical drawing exam and would then need to wait for another year to start university.

With my math and physics skills well developed, passing the exams to enter the university for electronics engineering was a breeze. It was easy to get a job after graduation in Romania in the 80s: simply choose from a list of jobs carefully curated by the university when it was your turn (depending on your results).

Thinking that a corporation would be ideal for me, I chose the national telecom company. And I worked there for eighteen years, changing departments every 3-4 years, to the disdain of those who thought you should stay in one department until you got a leadership role.

It was common thinking in Romania back then. But not for a person like me, curious to find things to do that she likes more.

When the company offered IT courses, I didn't think twice. And I discovered how natural it comes to me to learn anything in this field. I was right: you can do creative things if you're on the designing/programming side.

I was interested in a career change outside of the technical field even before coming to Canada in 2003. My creative soul was not happy in the telecom industry (engineering, in general). But I didn't know in which direction to go.

In 2002, I dislocated my right knee in a skiing accident. Bedridden for three months, slowly recovering …

One morning, I woke up in tears from a vivid dream, with a clear thought in my mind: "I have to go to Canada."

I took it as a sign from life—that it was the best move for me at that moment—since I'd given up the immigration idea two years earlier and never thought of it all that time. When I arrived in Canada, my knee was not fully recovered. But who cared? I trusted that sign; it motivated me to go through the immigration process and gave me courage to start over in a new country.

Four months after landing in Toronto as a permanent resident, I got an engineering position in the Quality Assurance department of a big company. Although I didn't enjoy working in this field, I thought it was a good move until I figured out my new career direction. I worked there for three years, putting my previous experience to good use. It also helped me develop new skills and gave me time to adapt to the new environment.

What does my experience in the technical field have to do with building the Introverts Academy?

First, I never agreed with those who said that I wasted all those engineering years when I shifted to a different career. That engineering experience taught me good lessons and enhanced my skills, which now help me build the Introverts Academy: strategizing, planning, implementation, dealing with complex problems, analytical thinking, risk management, creative problem solving, working with computers, focusing on high-quality products and services, professional communication, dealing with contractors ... Also, quality assurance tools like metrics and mind maps (which I now often use when I start a new project to brainstorm, strategize, and find solutions or ways for improvement).

The New Direction

During my first two weeks in Canada, I met two professional coaches on different occasions . Coincidence? Serendipity?

"What's coaching?" I asked the first one, the leader of a job search workshop I attended (to learn about the new professional environment into which I was tiptoeing). "I never heard of this profession in Romania."

The second coach was a statistician turned photographer and coach, which I met at the National Women's Show. Her postcards with beautiful nature photography caught my eye, since that's one of my hobbies. I was glad she opened the conversation, as I (an introvert) wouldn't have the courage to.

That experience made me discover the *networking* concept I kept hearing about in that workshop. And showed me a genuine way to tap into its benefits: focus on something you have in common when you approach people. That makes it easier to have a conversation, and—who knows—maybe you will discover more. As I did: it made me realize that Canada is a country where people can change directions at any age without feeling judged or needing to explain why. I loved that. It was so encouraging!

Three years went by until I felt settled enough in the Canadian environment and comfortable enough to *attack* a career change. I still didn't know in which direction, but all this time I kept adding items to a list of skills and things *I'd love* and *I want to avoid* in the career of my dreams.

The day I signed the contract to buy my condo apartment, I looked at my list. While scrolling down ... and up ... and down ... several times, one word popped into my mind: coaching. It triggered memories of the two coaches I'd met when I just landed here. I totally forgot about them and coaching since.

Was it life sending me another sign?

Determined to verify, I reached out to them both and asked more about coaching as a profession and what training is required. It turned out they both went through the same training, although they didn't know each other. "That's definitely a sign," I thought, and enrolled in the same coaching training. After the first day, I was hooked: coaching matches my personality so well, I hardly believed it.

The rest is history, as some might say. I started my coaching business while still in training, something they'd encouraged us to do—to keep practising the new skills and gain experience.

For several months, I wondered: "How can I make a smooth transition from engineering to coaching while waiting for my business to gain enough momentum to sustain me?"

Life sent me the answer via a coaching colleague. During a break, when I shared with her my dilemma, she quickly replied: "Humber College has a mentoring coach position for helping professional newcomers. It looks like a good match for your skills." Ding!

I didn't get that position, but I applied for and got another one: bilingual program coordinator for a mentoring program that helps professional newcomers. Since it was a new program, I loved that I could rely on my coaching, strategic, and creative skills to design and implement it. Also, I could use my French. "Why be trilingual if you can't use at least two languages in your job?"

Excited about the meaningful path waiting for me, I said *goodbye* to the engineering field.

I was tired of a profession with such rapid growth—requiring frequent updates and keeping up with new discoveries. I was longing for something where my creative spirit would feel more at ease. A profession where I could help people learn *how to fish* (find what they need) instead of relying only on external input (which usually makes us feel that we're never enough). A way to reveal the human potential in a world that came to value external information more. Glad that I found this profession!

Years of working in the technical field, in the corporate world, made me become quite a serious person, disengaged from her feelings. However, applying coaching to myself became a blessing.

I'll let a client's words describe the transformation she experienced from my coaching, because I felt the same: "*It stunned me to discover that my self-esteem was in time shattered by the negativities that surrounded me. The coaching increased my self-esteem, brought me inner peace, and answers for many problems. I rediscovered myself.*"

Being coached also helped me feel alive again, gain a sense of humour, and encouraged me to step up for myself more often. I became a *sponge*, eager to learn and gain more experience in this field … while helping others benefit from it. I gained more courage and learned valuable coaching techniques that helped me walk on this unknown, mysterious path. Many people who knew me disagreed with my new career choice. But deep inside, I felt it was the right path for me, and I trusted that gut feeling.

At one point, I remembered the psychology manual I bought in high school—although psychology was no longer part of the school or university curriculum due to changes in the educational system in Romania of those times. Since professional coaching is based on psychology, was buying that manual another sign from life for me?

However, I'm happy that I didn't look more into that path back then. I like the coaching approach more: it considers people to be naturally creative, resourceful, and whole. It helps them to go from where they are to where they want to be by removing the inner blockages and finding creative ways to overcome challenges and external roadblocks. It's a more empowering approach.

Back to my latest project:

Are sixteen years of coaching experience enough to add coaching services to the Introverts Academy?

I think they are. Especially since many of my individual clients were introverts. The organizations I helped (through system coaching) have introverts among their employees and need a workplace culture that allows both introverts and extroverts to thrive while contributing to the company's objectives.

The Training Skills

I never thought I'd become what some would call a *trainer*, *teacher*, or *university instructor*. I always believed this required being very knowledgeable in a field and pushing people to learn or telling them what to do. That's so far from what I want to do.

However, I ended up being called *trainer*, *teacher*, and *university instructor*—although what I really do comes from a different perspective. My *teaching* style (for lack of a better word) is highly interactive and experiential, using hands-on *training* focused on actual situations relevant to participants and their situations. I prefer to use a self-discovery process based on coaching techniques to help people learn something from my workshops, webinars, or courses. I share concepts that increase participants' awareness, spark their curiosity, encourage them to define or choose their own strategies, and find answers to their specific situation. I love this coaching approach. I experienced its benefits myself (that's how my coaching training was).

Being a free spirit, affecting other people's lives by pushing information *down their throat* or telling them what they must do, is something I avoid—since imposing information and strategies can make them doubt their own intuition or take away their free will.

As an introvert, I wasn't always comfortable speaking to several people at once. It was even worse when I had to cover topics in which I was not really interested, during workplace meetings, for example. My voice trembled when I had to speak with someone who I perceived to have an authority position.

However, when coaching became part of my life, I got an urge to help more people at once. So I started designing and delivering workshops. Another signal that life sent me?

Since I designed workshops on topics I was interested in, taking on the leadership role became less scary. And using a collaborative, interactive, and experiential facilitation style—which worked well with my introversion—put me more at ease.

First, I offered to do a workshop for an organization. And I survived and learned from that experience. In time, it became easier to do these workshops, and my confidence in public speaking increased. This also led to the opportunity to become a university instructor for a Business Communication course—which I designed, incorporating coaching concepts and techniques.

What I loved the most about such workshops (or webinars during the pandemic): I could use my expertise and creativity (to design them), and my system coaching skills (to create a supportive and nurturing environment that encourages self-expression and participation in the experiential exercises). An environment that suits introverts as well.

At one point, I took courses for adult learning and curriculum development. And, to the surprise of the instructor and me, I discovered that I already had those skills ... built through experience. Which reinforced my confidence and the belief that self-taught skills are as valuable as those learned in a traditional educational environment.

Was life preparing me along the way to enhance my public speaking, teaching, and facilitation skills? Probably. They are certainly useful for building the Introverts Academy.

Introversion vs. Extroversion

My mind says that I should have started with this topic, since it's directly related to the Introverts Academy's mission. However, my intuition didn't agree.

Since I started to listen again to my intuition, I discovered that it is always right so long as I capture its message, double check with it while I am in a calm state, and I'm patient to understand (in time) why it gave me the message.

Does this have something to do with introversion?

I think it does. Since the natural tendency for introverts is to focus more on their inner world, paying attention to intuition comes easily to them. However, living in a world that constantly bombards us with information and demands our attention could distract us from our intuition's gentle nudges.

I believe that intuition is one of life's ways of *speaking* to us. So I was happy when coaching helped me declutter the connection with my intuition—so I understand its messages more accurately.

Although I've always been an introvert (we're born this way), I discovered the concepts of introversion and extroversion only in my forties. I was already in Canada when I took the MBTI® (Myers-Briggs Type Indicator®) test during a training paid by the company I worked for.

That happened during my transition from engineering to coaching, and it was exciting to get confirmation that the path I've intuitively chosen was the right direction for me. Coaching matches well with my test results (INFP).

Learning more about introversion and extroversion was quite revealing. It helped me understand better my interactions with others.

Having an extroverted sister, over time I intuitively built coping mechanisms to deal with her innate behaviour; like withdrawing when I felt overwhelmed and taking time to recharge. But it wasn't easy. Remembering our interactions throughout the years—from the perspective of the introvert and extrovert innate complementary traits—it made more sense and increased my empathy with extroverts.

For ten years, I helped thousands of professionals by applying a coaching approach to job search and career development and combining it with my learning from working in various fields and sectors. A life experience that I came to accept and cherished. It was meaningful, rewarding, and creative.

At the beginning, it was fascinating to discover the distinct challenges faced by introverted and extroverted job seekers. And to realize that most strategies shared in books, and by employment and career counsellors, were of the *one solution fits all* type—instead of being customized to take advantage of the complementary innate strengths of introverts and extroverts.

It was understandable, in a way. The professional world is more aware of the extroverted behaviour and appreciates it (at least in North America).

However, understanding something doesn't mean it's right or it couldn't be better.

When I adapted the job search strategies for introverts and extroverts to work with their specific strengths and motivation triggers, my clients became more successful. To help more people at the same time, I designed and delivered workshops where both introverts and extroverts learned from each other about how different their behaviours are, and what strategies and tactics better fit their temperament traits.

One workshop, in particular, gave me a big AHA moment. For the forty university students, I set up the room with chairs in a circle. That's my preferred way to deliver workshops since they can see and learn from each other. And I can use the space in the middle for experiential exercises. Although it wasn't the first time I delivered the workshop *How Your Mindset Affects Your Job Search Results,* at one point I was inspired to ask: "How many of you are shy or introverted?"

Half of them raised their hands. I invited them to look around to see how others responded. Then I shared that I too used to be like this, but I worked on myself and now I had no problem leading workshops and speaking to strangers.

A student approached me after the workshop: "I'd like to thank you. The moment you asked us to look around, I realized that I'm not the only shy person in the world. And when you mentioned that you overcame your challenges, it gave me hope that I can overcome mine." Her words gave me goosebumps. Immediately, a thought crossed my mind: "I wonder how many introverts in the world feel like this, believing they're alone in a world full of extroverts? What would the world look like if more introverts become aware of that *bubble*, burst it, and focus instead on building their dream life and career?"

Was it life that brought the question to my mind?

I believe so. I felt like it's part of my life's purpose. And from that point on, I brought the concepts of introversion and extroversion into everything I did (workshops, webinars, coaching).

There's a danger of being passionate about something and working on it: you can ignore or minimize your body's alarm signals. Been there, done that in 2016. I was doing workshops every day and speaking with clients before and after. It was too much for an introvert. I didn't realize the toll this put on my body. And when I did, I thought I could still handle it. But the alarming signals piled up quickly, to a point that I couldn't work anymore. Nor talk … for four months.

Worried, I asked myself one day: "What will I do for the rest of my life if I can't talk anymore? I still want to help people." The answer came with the next thought: "Write a job search guide for introverts." Life showed me the way again, according to its plan for me.

"Smart move!" I thought. Besides making sense (I had a decade of experience in this field by then), it was a way to reach more people without spending my energy interacting with each of them.

Although I never thought of writing such a book, I gladly embraced this project. It gave me something to focus on when the world seemed to fall apart for me. This book project—besides helping many introverts since I published it—also facilitated my recovery from the burnout, and brought me the title *bestselling and award-winning author*. Plus, learning how to self-publish encouraged me to write and publish more books.

Along with my professional background and the strategies for introverts I've developed over time, the research I've done for this book has also been an eye-opener. For example, discovering a report from Psychometrics Canada (based on 58,000 MBTI® tests) which revealed that 48% of respondents are introverts.

So we're not a small percentage of the population.

Although introverts don't talk as much or interact as often as extroverts, that doesn't mean we don't exist or that our strengths aren't valuable. This keeps me motivated to build the Introvert Academy: to make more people aware of what I've learned about the valuable strengths of introverts and how they and the world can benefit more from them.

Content Creation

A project like Introverts Academy requires a lot of content, in various formats. And skills like curriculum design, image and video editing, graphic design, text editing …

Fortunately, I had already gained expertise in various fields and developed such skills before this project idea came to my mind. Thank you, life!

In Romania, I met someone (serendipity?) who had a digital camera while others were still using film cameras. I loved so much the idea of getting immediate access to photos that I bought a used digital camera as soon as I had the chance. I credit my hiking friends for giving me courage to share my nature photography with others. That meant becoming familiar with photo editing software. Challenge accepted!

I have taken many photographs since and, after I got into coaching, I combined these two (photography and coaching) in a photo-coaching album, to be used for self coaching. It was before Instagram. And after I learned to self-publish, that album became the first in the photo-coaching book series (also listed on the Introverts Academy website).

Once I got my hands into image editing software, graphic design was the next step. I like to design things, it's creative. At one point I even considered taking courses to become a graphic designer, but again my intuition didn't agree: "These are just skills you need to serve a bigger purpose, not to make a career."

These days is easier to create and adjust images online or with apps—for most of the website, marketing, and social media needs. However, I still use GIMP (similar to Photoshop) when the features of apps and online image editors are not enough. And when my skills don't rise to the level I want, there are plenty of contractors happy to lend their expertise to my project. Text editing, for example; I prefer to let others do their magic on editing my books.

"The need teaches you," says a Romanian proverb. When I started my coaching business, I didn't have money for website design. However, since I love anything IT, I challenged myself to design one. That way, I could update it when needed (which happened often). It got easier over time, with all the features WordPress has since developed. Another helpful skill to have for Introverts Academy.

Do Life Skills Count?

When I designed the mentoring program for professionals, I introduced a life coaching tool called *Wheel of Life*. It's a holistic approach that helps people to better understand where they are and how they can improve their life, by assessing it from different perspectives. I also designed and added a *Wheel of Job Search*, inspired by the same holistic approach. These tools became an effective way to help clients open up, identify their limiting beliefs regarding job search, and become curious about what else they can do to positively affect their results.

When the thought of starting the Introverts Academy came to me, lots of ideas followed quickly—as if they were waiting in a hidden place, ready to rush out into reality. I channelled them on paper using a mind map and the holistic approach I talked about earlier. That's how the Introverts Academy curriculum for individuals came to life, because I wanted it to be more than just about career or entrepreneurship for introverts.

People often think of their personal and professional lives as being separate. However, they influence each other, as strengths in one area can help the other.

Same with the weaknesses, but their impact can be minimized by using strategies that rely more on our strengths. My first book (*Introverts: Leverage Your Strengths for an Effective Job Search*) approached job hunting from this perspective.

So, do life skills count?

Yes, they do.

For example, my curiosity and openness to follow my intuition —when I transitioned from engineering to coaching—led to a professional path that I deeply enjoy, despite the rollercoaster it took me through. It wasn't always easy. But even the down moments came with important lessons. That's why I call my burnout experience, a *blessing in disguise*.

When I was taking the coaching courses, a friend insisted I go with her to Chicago for a two-day personal growth workshop (she could bring a guest). "We can take turns driving all night, and we'll get there in time," she said. Nine hours of driving one way from Toronto to Chicago just to attend a workshop? No way! I loved what I was learning in my courses; it was enough, I thought.

Two weeks later, she reached out again: "Come on, let's go together. We can drive your cute yellow car. You're already familiar with it."

It wasn't her words that convinced me. I took her persistence as a sign that life wanted me to go. So we went to what became … the first step to opening up my spiritual journey. In the following two years, I attended more similar workshops in the United States—in parallel with my coaching training. They complemented very well each other, helping me understand life and human behaviour at a deeper level … which benefited my coaching.

Around the same time, I started a daily meditation practice—which became another resourceful experience. In time, my mind got used to staying calm even outside the meditation. That was useful in keeping negative thoughts at bay, which had a positive effect on my energy level. It didn't get drained as much, so I became more productive. My creativity increased as well; with a calm mind, there was nothing left to block the creative flow. My observation skills sharpened, and I became more attuned to my intuition—both useful elements for coaching.

Soon after, I had two art photography exhibitions and received grants from the Ontario Arts Council. I also started to paint intuitively (and had a painting exhibition), and I designed artsy jewelry.

While I enjoyed that burst of creativity, life had other plans for me. It pushed me into the burnout that led to writing books for and about introverts. And later, to start the Introverts Academy. Which leads me to …

The Business Skills

I wanted to leave the technical field even before immigrating to Canada. So, when the opportunity showed up, I jumped on the chance to do an MBA with European Union funding. I was curious if that would be something I might be interested in.

"I'll do an MBA after I get a management position," a colleague said when I shared my plan with him. "Well, I'm doing it now to be ready for when I'll get such a position," I quickly replied, surprised by my own words. Where did they come from? Life pushed me into doing this as well?

While that MBA opened my mind to the interdependent relationships between the various departments of a company, it also increased my frustration. I could see many ways for improvement in the company I was working for, although I didn't have the ability to change things from the level I was at. The MBA also made me realize that becoming a manager in the corporate world didn't appeal to me.

Those business skills though (mission, vision, values, planning, operations, financials, marketing), and the big picture thinking the MBA came with, became valuable when I started my coaching practice.

And even when I published my first book. I considered it a product and applied business skills to this book project, to build momentum before and during the book launch, and continued to promote it after.

I felt an urge to write and get that book into the readers' hands as soon as possible, so I used all my skills to help achieve that aim. Did my life's purpose push me to do that?

These business skills are definitely helpful in building the Introvert Academy.

Armed with patience, I trust that I'm guided—step by step—to reach the purpose I was meant to fulfill.

· · ·

What about you?

Do you pay attention to the signs and experiences that life[1] pushes you through?

And do you allow them to guide you?

---

1. I call it *life*. Others might say God, the Universe, higher self, universal consciousness, or something else.

ABOUT THE AUTHOR

Gabriela Casineanu

Previous contributor to an IWA anthology

Gabriela Casineanu is an award-winning author, professional coach, university instructor, and artist. Like many Romanians, she started her professional path in engineering, but her creative and curious soul found a way to turn things around.

After immigrating to Canada, her career change to coaching opened exciting opportunities.

Forced by a burnout that affected her ability to speak for four months, Gabriela began writing in 2016. Author of eleven books (some translated into French and Romanian), she founded the *Immigrant Writers Association (IWA)* in 2018. An introvert passionate about creating a better world by tapping into introvert strengths, she now builds the *Introverts Academy*.

Connect with Gabriela Casineanu:

- Gabrielacasineanu.com
- Introvertsacademy.org

OUR MIGRATION JOURNEYS IN CANADA

BY ALKA KUMAR

Part One – Call me Sisyphus

On some days, if asked my name I want to say 'Sisyphus.' You may be aware of the famous story about Sisyphus, the King of Corinth as Greek legend has it, and as Wikipedia confirms. Punished by the gods for his deceit and craftiness, Sisyphus was condemned to roll a heavy boulder up a hill for eternity, and each time he almost reached the top, the boulder would roll back again and he would have to start over. It is right from the heart of that mythical story that the notion of an impossible task emerges. (There are other messages inherent in this mythical story, relating perhaps to punishment, overreach, justice, and other moral conundrums, but for now let us stay with this theme—perseverance in the face of impossibility.)

The Sisyphus story, then, could be a metaphor for a situation where individuals find themselves in the midst of circumstances where the odds are stacked heavily against them, and they have no option but to swim against the tide. In fact, life demands of them that they act in complete contradiction even to the laws of nature, including the very force of gravity. Such a Sisyphean predicament can easily lead an individual to experience despair and feel trapped forever in a loop of hope-lessness, with no pathways open for escape.

Why do I tell this story as an opener to my reflections on 'finding the way,' you may well ask! Well, our lives are full of stories—of birth, death, relationships, and other important life tropes; in fact, as humans, we are at one level storied versions of ourselves, just as stories are containers often holding universal truths that are at the heart of our experiences. Also, stories can be the bridge that connects us with each other. The Sisyphus story can then be my story, or it might be yours, as the common denominator in the human predicament is that our lives are lived in the grey spaces between happy and sad, good and evil, success and failure. In the ultimate analysis, isn't the game of life about navigating troubled waters in the best ways we can and staying afloat, using all the tools in our toolbox of life?

For me, the Sisyphus story is an important reminder of the experiences shared with me by many of my clients and research participants—individuals often categorized (and perceived) as 'newcomers' or 'immigrants,' regardless when they arrived in Canada. While categories are often needed, they can also become labels that never leave us; sadly, and oftentimes, individuals who have lived here most of their lives still get 'seen' through a kind of 'outsider' lens based on our skin colour, the accent in our speech, or cultural markers such as our clothing, customs, or religious practices. The Sisyphus story can also be interpreted as a way to acknowledge an indi-vidual's persistence and fortitude, and of their superhuman ability to keep hope alive in the face of utter loss. In my roles as a career development and employment coach, and as mentor in the immigrant settlement sector—with foreign trained professionals and with newcomer and refugee youth —I have met many stories that demonstrate just these tensions between dealing with adversity and trying to find the light, between feeling lost and finding that elusive and difficult way.

First, a snapshot of me—and a small window into my story— to ground this bigger narrative about finding the way. My spouse and I first landed in Manitoba in 2007, on one of those Winnipeg nights in mid-February when it's minus 40 degrees Celsius. Despite a few years of preparation, we found ourselves barely ready for what we encountered. How did I expect to be ready for these sub-zero temperatures, coming as I did from tropical climes, with the humid, plus-40 summers of New Delhi being more the norm for me? I still remember my first morning in Winterpeg (endearingly named so, by locals and others, for obvious reasons), when a friend picked me up at the hotel and took me for a drive around the city, and I saw Assiniboine Park all magical in its pristine white beauty under an expansive prairie sky. The beautiful carpet of summer grass I saw in this park a few months later was nowhere in sight on my first visit here. Right now, what I was seeing looked more like a frozen ocean or a giant skating rink, and I asked my friend with some wonder, "Is this a park, really?" And she offered in response, "Yes, in the summer, it's also a cricket field, we have many cricket enthusiasts, even competing teams here, did you know that?" No, I certainly did not. I knew then that this brand- new phase of my life journey would contain many unknowns.

Finding a job in Winnipeg was no cakewalk as I had no clue where to even start. Back home in Delhi, as an academic for most of my previous life, all I was trained for was teaching and research. I had never worked in retail or in a bank, in a coffee shop or a call centre, or indeed in any sector other than education, and teaching and learning made up my entire world. Being in a time and geographical space where the cultural norms were quite different, it was fairly normal to get that first job and stay with it till the day you retired. Of course, in my tenured position at the university, in addition to teaching and research, I performed several other everyday tasks—like grading and mentoring students; designing under-graduate and graduate courses as well as other educational curricula and exam papers; and organizing seminars, confer-ences, and other discussions. I gave talks here and there, and wrote for academic and non-academic publications.

Do take note, dear reader, that in my introduction above, I have instinctively prefaced my life and my professional identity with the words, 'all I was trained for.' When I reflect on this turn of phrase that came to me so spontaneously, awareness begins to dawn that this is actually a lot of life lived optimally, as well as experience and expertise gathered with love, dedica-tion, and passion. This was the gift package of life I carried with me everywhere I went. And that's not all. Let's not forget, this past life was also what gave me the core sense of my iden-tity. It made me who I was, and all these experiences have shaped the person I am today. This is also the in-essence person I will always be, hopefully with more layers of under-standing, learning, and growth added on as I move through my kaleidoscopic life.

Once I was done with my sad musings at the irony in my self-deprecating statement 'all I was trained for,' I suddenly real-ized how easily I had dismissed myself. This was the lightbulb moment making me aware that I was discounting the gifts I was bringing to the table. If I, knowing myself to be good at what I do, and loving my work with all-consuming intensity as well as having the experience and self-assurance to do anything I was tasked with, could play down my own strengths when I knew them so well, why was I blaming employers, interviewers, and evaluation processes in Canada for doing the same to me and to my clients? I suddenly realized that in buying into the perceptions and assumptions of others as to who I was, I had allowed myself to lose my confidence. Being new in a country and a city where things were done quite differently from what I was used to, my self-esteem had not just plummeted, it had disappeared! These feelings were made worse by the lack of response I received to several targeted and well-presented resumes that I submitted. Yes, I was doing it all the right way too—as recommended, I was indeed tweaking my master resume document each time to customize it in accordance with every position I saw.

I was advised to do this by experienced professionals in the settlement sector who also told me that neither who I was, nor the educational and work experience I carried with me, would be enough when I went out looking for my dream job here in Canada. That in fact, not only was my lack of Canadian experience a problem, but that the PhD I had in English would be a liability rather than an asset; I was advised to take it out of my resume. (This I refused to do as it seemed dishonest for many reasons that I should perhaps write about elsewhere!) They also offered me the alarming statistic that more than 80% of the job market is hidden (true) and cannot be accessed unless you have 'social capital.' This term, in case you're wondering, signifies the social and professional networks an individual is a member of, and it is quite natural that when you are new in a country or a city, it takes time to get to know people, form new relationships, and develop mutual trust. The only way to acquire social capital, much needed for accessing professional opportunities, is through aggressive networking, I was told. This in turn meant being always ready with some version of that dreaded 'elevator pitch.' For introverts, such a task can be positively daunting, and even for those of us who are extroverts, certain environments can still feel overwhelming, leading easily to stage fright; and that is not the best-case scenario when it comes to elevator pitches! And believe me—in case this is something you have not experienced personally—it is so easy to feel like a failure simply by messing up that golden opportunity to share appropriately your 'who you are' speech with people on whom you want to make a good first impression.

Given the above overall context, imagine now that you have waited endlessly for that interview call you want so badly—isn't it natural for self-doubt to creep in, leading to paralysis and exhaustion, even deep discouragement? For myself, I know from key moments in my past when I had moved forward in my life and attained my goals, it had all happened for me when the path ahead was clearly visible, and I felt strong and confident, excited and curious. And now—being in this unfamiliar new country, and not getting any opportunities to do what I loved or be who I believed I was—the path ahead looked foggy and treacherous, and I had no idea how to proceed. Was I not trying hard enough, and should I be pushing myself further? Or was I simply not good enough? While such questions assailed me, my circumstances made me feel like Sisyphus with his onerous boulder, and I felt as if the responsibility to do better was all on me. However, instead of pushing harder, I was losing the drive I previously had, and the momentum. Worse still, I felt my positive energy ebbing away and my indomitable spirit slowly eroding. Was I then the one standing in my own way, blocking my own path towards progress?

All this self-criticism was already bad enough, but it was made even worse by those who encouraged me not to be over-whelmed, urging me instead to be resilient. I was asked to empower myself and never be fazed by what stands in my way. When I was told I could do this, the words sounded empty and hollow—how could I believe them? Nobody really shared the complex recipe I could use to cook this secret sauce of resilience. I don't blame them as so many ingredients are needed to do this, and the proportion in which these need to be mixed varies too. The timing too must be perfect as each of us is as unique as are our careers and life pathways. This makes it doubly challenging to come up with cookie-cutter solutions to our problems, be they personal or professional.

Part Two – Searching for the Way

In this second section, I share some of the key learnings from my research and front-line work with internationally educated immigrants in Canada, but before I do that, let me give you a few glimpses from their lives. In one of the interviews I conducted for my qualitative research study, on how racialized skilled immigrants experience their job market integration in Winnipeg, it was heartbreaking to hear X observe, "They didn't even give me the opportunity to fail." Y shared, "I've knocked on so many doors, but somehow it's always the wrong one." In one of the focus groups I ran, I asked S to describe how she felt now that she had been in Canada for two years. Her response, and her lacklustre eyes, left me depressed for the rest of the day. She said, "It feels as if I'm blindfolded, I feel like a blind kitten. And mind you, I was supervising a team of nearly fifty back home in my last job." R had been in Canada for nearly three years, and apart from taking a couple of bridging courses and volunteering in hopes of getting that proverbial 'foot in the door,' his main job at this time was to search for employment that had potential for a career, not any job but the one he believed was the right one for him. When I asked what success meant to him, he became thoughtful and then responded, "Success is about adding value to yourself, and significance is about adding value to others." Clearly, and as he expanded later, when he shared his professional life story, his conceptualization of such a response came from the work he did in his pre-migration life, as a leader and a mentor in his field and a role model whose sense of purpose came from not just focusing on his own achievements, but from uplifting others and helping them grow. Unfortunately, so many factors become variables—including life experiences individuals have had in their home country that shape their current expectations—that might lead them to experiencing success or failure in certain ways; and these factors carry the potential to impact individuals uniquely and specifically, so it's not easy to come up with standard templates for finding their way.

So where does that leave us? If we and our problems are so different from each other, how can we take lessons from others' stories and apply them to our own situation to find the way? (This is where community networks and talking to each other can help; research helps too, but more on that another time!) Speaking specifically about the issue of seeking employment for skilled immigrants and newcomers in Canada if they are non-white and racially diverse, we can observe that despite and beyond differences that exist between individuals and groups, shared commonalities do exist. Even a quick read of the four accounts presented above—experiences narrated by my research participants—indicate commonalities in the obstacles they experienced. For instance, for job seekers, it is problematic that despite having 'human capital' on the basis of which they acquire permanent residency in Canada, their efforts at finding employment they are trained for are often not easy or successful; and this means they do not get to have that first crack at a job where they could showcase what they can do or who they are. When this happens, not only is this a blow to an individual's self-esteem, it also impedes the process of being the professional they aspired to be in their new home; and such a scenario leads to an absence of belonging and a feeling of lacking active citizenship. Looking at the second account closely, if every door someone is knocking on turns out to be the wrong one, this could potentially indicate structural issues where the odds stacked against an individual are many, and they are complex, which makes the situation a challenging and intractable one. It is clear that they are trying hard as they have taken the initiative to try many avenues, applying multiple strategies to seek solutions. The metaphor used in the third account—'feeling like a blind kitten'—is compelling and resonant, and it reiterates the failures embedded in the newcomer settlement and integration ecosystem where the many pieces of the puzzle could (should) be better aligned, so that services may be coordinated and streamlined more efficiently, carrying the potential to be received as seamless and responsive from the perspective of the individual. This may lead to outcomes that are more desirable, again, from the standpoint of the individual, not only from that of the state. The last quote—that differentiates 'success' from 'significance'—I find simultaneously inspirational and heartbreaking. It demonstrates to me the losses being incurred every day—both by the individual and by the state—when potential hires capable of articulating their experiences and aspirations in this manner do not get opportunities to contribute to the economy and the country and do not find the professional environment they need for self-actualization. There is no dearth of available academic literature or anecdotal evidence in the labour market integration context to confirm scenarios similar to the ones I cite above. The good thing about the migration experience is that it's a shared one, and it's everywhere, in us and around us, including perspectives that provide generational snapshots. These hidden stories need to be told and heard and taken seriously; if lived experience is valued more, and spaces are created where voices of front-line staff-employment counsellors and career development practitioners, and others who support new immigrants in the job sector are amplified, these stories can be made more visible in the mainstream context. And then perhaps policy makers will take further note of the missing pieces that currently exacerbate barriers to economic integration for many individuals, groups, and communities.

Summarizing a few shared challenges that emerge from the accounts shared above—from my research findings, my front-line work with immigrants and newcomers, and my personal journey to find my own desired professional place—these stories starkly highlight the diminishment of confidence in individuals when they repeatedly encounter setbacks. For instance, they may get no interview calls in response to resumes they've submitted, or they may lack success in inter-views, or they may get that first job but then get laid off soon, all without understanding 'the why' in these decisions that impact them adversely. What happens next is logical, and for many who are already feeling diffident and unsure by now, they quickly attribute their lack of success to their lack of fluency in English, and/or they see their non-Canadian accent as a problem—can there be one single Canadian accent in a country of immigrants though? (We do know that apart from the many indigenous communities that are the original inhabi-tants of this land, the rest of the population of Canada is all immigrants from some part of the world.) In my experience, many assumptions—about being inadequate or imperfect due to a lack of fluency in English—are made by individuals even when they are actually really good communicators and likely have other qualifications and personal attributes that would make them excellent employees, given the chance. Besides, it helps that Canada's population is so diverse, and that ways to speak the English language are so varied, often heavily influ-enced by the intonations of our first languages. However, negative self-perceptions are easy to acquire based on how we are perceived by others, especially when the environment is unfamiliar and we don't understand how things work. These thoughts and feelings can be exacerbated when an individual is dealing with multiple challenges or uncertainties; or they may have timid, shy, diffident, or introverted personalities. Absence of the infamous Canadian Experience may be flagged by recruiters in many cases, or it takes forever more for licensing and credentialing processes to complete. These long waits are not easy, and the time taken can be demoralizing and damaging. The uncertainty can easily drain people of their energy and enthusiasm, their financial resources, and a lot more, leaving negative impacts on mental health.

Part Three – I will not be Sisyphus

The way we may be searching for could also be re-conceptualized as a series of small and interconnected journeys or directions that could potentially be taken; the initial one going towards a short-term goal, followed by a medium term one, and then one that is more long range; and based on the outcome of each small journey, decisions would need to be made regarding what the next move might be. Moreover, chances are that this way is not a linear pre-determined straight line external to the individual. (We build this pathway based on our attitudes, our experiences, and our actions.) Nor is it a clear horizontal road that can potentially join point A to point Z, rather it's often a broken meandering pathway where the road forks again and again, and individuals must decide which fork to take each time. Musing on this context often reminds me of Robert Frost's poem 'The Road Not Taken' (1916). If you don't know it, here it is:

Two roads diverged in a yellow wood,
And sorry I could not travel both
And be one traveler, long I stood
And looked down one as far as I could
To where it bent in the undergrowth;

Then took the other, as just as fair,
And having perhaps the better claim,
Because it was grassy and wanted wear;
Though as for that the passing there

Had worn them really about the same,

And both that morning equally lay
In leaves no step had trodden black.
Oh, I kept the first for another day!
Yet knowing how way leads on to way,
I doubted if I should ever come back.

I shall be telling this with a sigh
Somewhere ages and ages hence:
Two roads diverged in a wood, and I—
I took the one less traveled by,
And that has made all the difference.

I can easily imagine myself standing at that crossroads where the two roads diverge, and I see myself feeling uncertain about the one I should choose as there's no knowing where either would end up. Let's not forget the element of chance, or personal luck, that shows up unbidden in our lives as coincidence, as we don't know who that stranger might be who comes along and suggests some new course of action that might begin to open all doors that were so far closed. A mentor may be the instrument leading us to find the elusive way. However, this will only happen if we are open to receiving the gifts of serendipity, achievable through being willing to step outside our comfort zone.

Let's return to Sisyphus once more and ask ourselves to imagine what he might need by way of problem-solving tools that he could apply to his situation to find his way. He would have to begin with taking stock, learning in detail about both his barriers and what might be his likely options for solutions. For instance, could he get rid of that heavy boulder he was carrying up the mountain; could he make it smaller or lighter; could he find others who might help him by sharing his burden, perhaps? Maybe it was the steep incline of the mountain and the long journey to the top that he was finding unsurmountable, so could there be another path up and around the mountain that may be less steep and easier to navigate? These are barriers external to Sisyphus, but there may be others that are inside him that could be part of who he is, and these could be a part of the solutions too. For instance, if he's easily tired or gets out of breath, maybe he needs to build his strength or take frequent breaks for rest. Perhaps he needs a support infrastructure of cheerleaders who encourage him each time he feels he cannot go any further, and this might help him make it to the next milestone on his difficult journey.

Extrapolating from the Sisyphean predicament, it is clear that finding our way is, importantly, about starting with engaging with all aspects of the problem, being open and upfront when examining it, and breaking it down to its small but multiple components—both external and internal—and examining them each in detail so as to explore creative and innovative solutions. Doing this can help us learn about the problem and shine a light on who we are and how we react in certain situations; what keeps us going and what pulls us back; and also, when we must reach out for help, and where and how we might find supportive community networks where relationships of mutual trust can develop. Fostering meaningful relationships is really key in this context as they can be psychologically strengthening and help us see that we're not alone, that it's not about an individual's inadequacy per se, but about the intersectional systemic issues here that create many of these hurdles in the first place.

Particularly in the case of intertwined labour market issues that collectively begin to appear overwhelming for newcomers, immigrants, and refugees, it is critical to understand equally well the ecosystem creating these challenges, and also one's own self. Going back to times in our lives when we felt in control, achieved success, or managed to move forward despite setbacks can be a good reminder of one's own capabilities. This can in turn help expand self-belief and our sense of self, such self-affirmations boosting confidence, suddenly leading to optimistic ways of thinking and a burst of positive energy. The migration experience causes disruptions, and it can create uncertainties making the landscape in the new country appear unfamiliar and strange. It is possible that despite all preparation, there is no prior frame of reference to understand this completely different context. This is how I experienced my new reality fifteen years ago when I first moved to Canada; and one of the factors that helped me cope with my unfamiliar environment was my ability to embrace the new with openness and curiosity. I learned quickly that there was no point resisting what was available by trying to chase fixed ideas of jobs I already knew how to do. If I did that, I would end up limiting my options, perhaps waiting endlessly, so why not be open to exploring something new as this might be my only chance to do so. It helped that such a way of thinking came naturally to me, and that it filled me with excitement. For many others, this may not be the case, and perhaps they spent a small number of magnificent early years in a particular profession back in their home country, and that's the only career path they would now like to pursue and excel in here in their new home. However, if a move to explore a new direction can be seen as a temporary strategic one under these changed circumstances, then individuals may end up feeling more in control of their actions, benefiting from a decision that may not have occurred or appealed to them instinctively. This, in and of itself, is a position of power from which to act, and it can lead to decision making in the future that includes taking some risks they may not have felt ready for earlier.

Finally, the individuals who shared their stories with me—the research participants who were part of my study, and the newcomer clients I worked with back then—believed and stated clearly that sharing their stories is essential as these can communicate key messages more widely.

One of their messages is that theirs is an uphill journey and that systems—organizations, institutions, leaders, and all levels of government—must respond to their needs if the promise of Canadian immigration made to them is to be actualized into active citizenship on the ground.

The second message is equally powerful: that as individuals, we cannot and will not accept the conditions of vulnerability thrust upon us, that we will not be Sisyphus. We will work diligently and continuously to achieve our goals, building our own capacities while valuing the assets we carried with us to our new home in Canada.

The processes of finding our way include supporting each other and advocating for ourselves and for our communities, creating leadership spaces where our lived experiences are valued and our bold voices are heard. And increasingly, finding the way is about resolutely creating it by charting a new path for ourselves, something that might also help others.

ABOUT THE AUTHOR

Alka Kumar

Alka Kumar, Ph.D., is a Research Affiliate with the Canada Excellence Research Chair in Migration and Integration at Toronto Metropolitan University.

With education and work experience in the humanities and in social sciences—literary studies, migration, and peace studies—Alka focuses her research and practice work in migration on building the overall capacity and leadership potential of individuals to help community-led initiatives flourish, and on strengthening inclusion and equity structures.

As a consultant, Alka supports immigrants and newcomers through teaching, writing, mentoring, and career transition counselling. She also works with organizations to develop DEI frameworks that help enhance community wellbeing.

Connect with Alka Kumar:

- alkakr436@gmail.com
- Linkedin.com/in/alka-kumar

MY WAY IS ... WRITING!

BY EMANUEL PETRESCU

This is by far the most complicated text I had to write. I'm unsure why because I got inspired doing the first draft; then, the second one was terrible.

In the spirit of the previous chapters I've written for the anthologies of Immigrant Writers Association (IWA), I'm listening to a song by *Dilated Peoples—Show Me The Way* featuring Aloe Blacc.

Because I know I need to find the way, but sometimes it needs to be shown.

This is the way—The Mandalorian.

First, I wanted to write a fiction story, as I started reading some over the past year. I've brainstormed a lot and brought up some old notes, but nothing seemed to make any sense—I guess I don't have enough discipline for it.

So I started *freestyling* like a HipHop emcee would—just start writing and see where it goes. And I did go somewhere indeed. I discovered that throughout my lifetime, I always found *my way* through writing.

If you're reading this, it's a confirmation.

The legend goes that when my baptism anniversary was celebrated (East European tradition), they came with a plate for me to choose different objects—which could represent the path I would choose in my life. A *pen* supposedly was one of the items I picked.

I never realized how much writing means to me until I wrote this text.

It goes back to my childhood when I learned the first letters. Soon after I knew the words, I started writing short, historical fiction stories. As I learned about some historical figures at school, I imagined different episodes—spinoffs as they call them in *Hollywood*—and started laying them on paper.

I still remember the pen I used to write those; for whatever reason, it was the other side of the eraser pen used to correct handwriting. I also remember the notebook—a math notebook that had a metal spiral and 80 pages—something not many had back then as most stationery was from the communist era.

These stories were no longer than 4 to 5 pages, and I only wish I could remember at least one.

I also remember how I didn't like to write on the left side (after you turned the page as that metal spiral was in my way), but soon it was brought to my attention that paper costs money and it's not to be wasted in that way.

The reason I remember the *pen* and *the paper* is that I was inspired by them.

Certain elements inspire me—pen and paper do that.

The position when writing is also important—the way the light casts shade—this is why in schools, most classrooms have the windows on the left. As most people are right-handed, the (natural) light doesn't create a shadow while they write.

But as I am sure many discovered, the shadow has certain "magic" that can add to the writing ...

The time of the day (or night) can also influence my writing —and how *I* write it. I'm still amazed how, all of sudden, based on the position and the pen I'm using, my handwriting becomes readable.

On what I'm writing is also important.

Recently I've discovered the North American yellow legal pads —the ones you only see in movies, usually used by attorneys. I used them to write notes during (virtual) meetings, as I instructed everyone to ensure they see me write things down. Otherwise, what I am supposed to do won't happen. Coupled with an adequate pen (a simple, cheaper one does the trick for me although I have way more fancy and expensive ones), those yellow pads indulge me in writing longer sentences.

The device I'm writing on matters to me.

I've been using a desktop PC for personal use for the past couple of years, which has been amazing for my sanity (you can't take the desktop to your bed). Also, for productivity—as I can only work on one while sitting at a desk, but it's not as inspiring when it comes to writing.

It seems that a laptop works best for writing (the first version of this chapter only appeared after I chose to write on my laptop). Especially on the older Macs, as the keyboard has, somehow, embedded already what I want to communicate and striking the keys comes naturally. I've tried the Apple keyboard and the new Apple laptops, and it's not the same.

Umberto Eco had a similar view if I remember correctly.

We could probably write a PhD thesis on keyboards. And someone probably did. I've purchased a premium set that everyone recommended but I'm not satisfied. My other $40 set from Walmart does a great job also.

Speaking of devices, it's becoming harder to write on smartphones—even text messages, not to mention emails or notes —but I remember how *productive* I was when I had a Blackberry (eons ago).

Back in my childhood, I could never write with ink. I get that there could be *magic* in the ritual of filling the fountain pen, but that magic is not for me.

Later came the fountain pen that held a reserve—a game-changer, as the grip on those pens was different. Handwritten letters, cards, and book covers were my favourite things to write with those types of pens.

Around the same time, I discovered the possibilities a solid pencil could bring. Especially the equivalents of the no. 2 pencils we saw in cartoons from North America.

Because, again, you need to consider the context: a post-communist period, where all stationery was communism branded—the pencils that used to break every time you sharpened them, the notebooks that smelled and felt dirty, and the fact that having a certain type of fountain pen could attract some unwanted attention, etc.

Suddenly, after 1990, we had access to a different culture and its tools. Stationery items were among these tools.

As for styles, journaling is one type of writing I started relatively early on. I still remember my first journal (and probably still have it somewhere); a fancy red-covered blank sheet notebook we (my family) got by subscribing to a book club. I had that for some time, but I started writing in it after my first library visit.

In my own language, we call a "library" a "bookstore," and for "bookstore" we use what you might translate as "bookshelf."

Fast forward twenty-something years later. After the "not so fun period" I mentioned in the my previously published chapters in IWA's anthologies, I started a separate "health" journal.

I received an award as the *employee of the month,* and among many other gifts was a notebook that said *I'm busy being awesome* on its cover.

I find it funny that my work and contribution were appreciated the most when I was at one of my lowest points.

That's why I decided to keep track of all my "states"— how I feel, why, what I ate and what the reaction was, etc. These tend to help because, after a while, I started seeing patterns, so I made adjustments to correct them.

What gets measured gets managed.—Peter Drucker

And it made sense to use that notebook for that.

Back in my childhood, after I started journaling, I probably filled tons of yearly agendas my mom used to bring home from work—filled with stories I invented based on plots from Batman, Superman, and other superheroes I encountered. Since we didn't have access to all the comic books that were available in other places (North America and Europe), I guess I had to invent my own.

I still laugh when after taking so much time to write some plots, I discovered that without the usage of diacritics (special Romanian characters), the translated names of some villains would become hilarious (for example *Mr. Freeze* became *Mr. Boot*—as in shoe).

I tried to write a comic at one point, but I didn't get past page 2 …

Not long after, I had a computer. And that was indeed a game changer. Besides games, I also had access to a text editor (actually Microsoft Word) that allowed me to come back and do corrections.

Grade 2 saw an intense effort from me and some of my colleagues as we launched an independent magazine where we mostly used to write short sci-fi stories we invented under the influence of Star Trek. Creating characters, plots, situations, and entire universes gave us a God-like status, even if just among ourselves.

This was a tremendous (and costly) effort on our end as printing just 1 page back then was not really accessible to anyone (think 1994-1995). I had access to a printer, and when that was not available, I tried printing the magazine using an old matrix one.

And when that was not available, I used the typewriter, stuck in some pictures cut up from different magazines or some hand drawings, and copied them via the copy machine —hardcore DTP.

Speaking of typewriters, I did have a couple throughout my lifetime, and I remember I brought one with me on a family trip to the mountains, feeling "inspired" by it. Not sure if you know, they do carry weight and can become quite noisy— hence not really good for relaxation time—for others, anyhow.

As with any successful publishing project, my colleagues and I had some disagreements. And I went and started writing reviews for computer games, something I used to play a lot back then (remember, this was in Eastern Europe in the early 1990's).

I fell in love with the "review" style as it lets you express feelings you wouldn't otherwise (also, picture that scene from the Mel Brooks movie with the first art critic of the world).

I still believe the outcome would have been different if we were in another place and another time. I don't think I was conscious of this then, but looking back, being appreciated by the *authorities* (the school) would have been nice.

Everything turned off (obviously, it didn't go away since you're reading this) sometime in the 7th grade when I spent some extra time writing a story the teacher asked us to do. Mine had like 10 or 12 pages, where most had two at the most. I was proud of the result and couldn't wait to read it in front of the class, mostly to hear my teacher's opinion.

I never had the chance since they sent us home for the class I was supposed to be reading it to. Kids do stuff, and we were no better. It was a warm spring day, and we decided to have a water fight, so we were all wet—hence the (solid) reason why they sent us home.

No one's fault, but I somehow thought the effort was not worth it.

Rarely any fiction after that.

Handwriting is an essential skill we tend to forget—hence these journaling exercises help with muscle memory. I say this because for the longest time I was under the impression that it was only I who experienced this.

And speaking of muscles, I had a couple of years when I hadn't written much by hand; you can imagine the soreness and the bitterness in my hand (and the entire arm) after I had to write a single page. Hint: it had to do with filling paperwork when I did some accounting.

Now, since I'm doing this constantly, I am better—at writing more, not better or more legible (as I believe no one can really read my handwriting). As said, I *sometimes* do.

I also recently discovered this 10-minute journaling technique that I do more and more every day. It's not exactly a to-do list —something I always have at hand; I call my real notebook *Asana* after a project management app I use.

Taking 10 minutes to disconnect and write down thoughts, ideas, or anything really, helps with my mindset—I start seeing things from a different perspective.

There are also the blogs I'm writing. I always said writing blogs is therapeutic (and way cheaper than therapy itself).

I've been writing in Romanian and English for more than ten years, constantly. I've started a couple of blogs—some are still around. In 2012 I started one in English, where I write mainly about the feelings and ideas that watching some movies trigger. I wouldn't call it a *movie review* because I often mention the film itself for only about 10%, the rest being memories or ideas I had while interacting with that film.

And I found myself writing there more and more; unexpectedly more, even today. Again, this is a fantastic exercise.

I also wrote (in Romanian originally, then translated it to English) an eBook about home recording. Technical, I know. It is still (as far as I know) the only eBook that talks about home recording in my native language. That eBook was accompanied by thousands of words of content in the form of web pages and blogs, social media posts, and newsletters for that project.

I ended up doing that project because I was involved in the underground music industry, and I've developed some skills I wanted to share (among other things I've developed are digital marketing skills, a field I'm active in today).

Besides the technical knowledge I developed and used to create content, in that period, I learned a lot about how to write press releases, pitch via emails, copy, and material for *the web*. I've written many press releases, titles, subject lines, descriptions, and social media posts—for each channel individually.

To an extent, I'm still learning how to write these things.

Gaining those skills got me working on other projects. And at one point, I was co-owner and editor of a self-development website (through a Christian point of view) where I've written at least a dozen (great—I believe) articles and newsletters.

Again, therapeutic.

But nothing moved the needle more than writing my blog—a public journal. And believe it or not, some people actually read what I wrote!!!

And from that, I've probably developed the habit of writing emails that are longer than usual—as anyone who has received an email from me might have noticed (or perhaps they had the impression they were reading a newsletter). I'm working on that, and since I have the *zero inbox* policy and some emails require an answer ASAP, I tend to send short messages now.

That's happening because I need to write them from my cell, and I don't like writing on a smartphone. Never did. I appreciate that I always have it on me and can access important documents, but I am not a fan.

Writing for IWA has been therapeutic as well. As said, I initially wanted to write a short fiction story for this anthology, but fiction is something I put aside a long time ago. It's been an extended period when I haven't read much fiction either, but I'm working on improving—because we need some fiction in our lives.

And one can watch only so much on *Netflix*. Better spend that time doing something else (I can't even watch a show anymore).

In 2021 I started sending my newsletter regularly (give or take). I should have started doing so 12 years ago, but who keeps track?

So writing was probably the only constant thing in my life. A way to reconnect with myself, heal, and find my way forward.

ABOUT THE AUTHOR

Emanuel Petrescu

Previous contributor to an IWA anthology

Originally from Romania, Emanuel Petrescu came to Canada in late 2016 and settled in Toronto with his wife.

Emanuel is an SEO consultant who helps businesses optimize their web presence to be more easily found on Google when users search for the products or services these businesses offer.

Personally, he is an eclectic individual who is passionate about writing, reading, innovative ideas, music (he was once a DJ), and getting to know as much as he can about many subjects. He has been actively involved with the Toastmasters organization.

Emanuel has contributed to three IWA anthologies and serves on its Board

Connect with Emanuel Petrescu:

- Emanuelp.com
- Howaboutsomemarketing.com

FINDING THE WAY

BY BRIAN SANKARSINGH

Part I – A History

Imran sits in the shadow of a pale blue moon, contemplating his life. Born to a Dalit, or untouchable, father and a Muslim mother, he did not fit in anywhere. Untouchables were members of the lowest social group in the Hindu caste system. The word Dalit itself meant broken and was the name they gave themselves in the 1930s.

Situated in the southeast part of Iran, Sistan and Baluchestan is widely considered the poorest province. Deep historical lines of division were drawn between Muslims and Hindus, and Imran was born in '*No Man's Land.*'

In the Muslim area of town, he was spurned because his mother had the temerity to marry a Hindu. In the smaller and even humbler Hindu shantytown, he was ostracized because of his low caste.

His stomach signals its emptiness with a loud audible gurgle. Ignoring this distraction, Imran continues writing as the moon peeps hesitantly through the clouds.

It is his poetry that helps him survive and cope; he uses it to express the eternal hope that burns in his heart and diminish the cold sadness that lives alongside it. Little does Imran know that his penchant for sneaking out to sit under the old oak tree to look up at the stars and write would one day save his life.

She shuns me like the
Upper caste avoids
The untouchable
I reach for her, and she
Jumps out of her skin with
Palpable fear
Tangible repugnance
Visible revulsion

Oh, how I wish I could
Once more feel the passion
Of her exquisite gaze
I writhe in feverish frenzy
Caught in a delirious haze
I compel myself to squeeze
Shut my eyes

Perhaps now,
She will approach
Silent footfalls
Sweet
Blissful
Sleep

Part II – New Beginnings

Sitting in his one-room apartment in the attic of a house in Toronto's Parkdale neighbourhood, Imran reflects on the journey that brought him here.

After receiving several threats of violence and murder, he escaped to Canada as a Convention Refugee. He had very little money and no idea what to expect, but this was his chance for a new beginning. All his worldly possessions were neatly packed into an unassuming worn-out leather suitcase. For a fleeting moment, Imran pensively gazes out his tiny window. The calmness of Lake Ontario is juxtaposed by the incessant drone of tires on the Gardiner Expressway. When he first arrived, he wondered if he would ever get used to that sound. Now, he barely notices it. In fact, many nights it lulls him to sleep.

Unceasing
Monotonous
Repetitive droning

Nameless lives
Conveyed to and fro
In multitudinous metal bubbles

How interesting those lives must be
Filled with purpose
Saturated with intent

Secure in their future
Soothing serendipity
In mechanical monotony

Months turn into years in the flicker of an eye. Imran is sitting in the back of the King Street streetcar. His body sways back and forth in time with the movement of the streetcar. A smile plays across his face as he looks out the window.

He is tired, having just completed two consecutive shifts at his part-time job, but he is energized with excitement. His only childhood friend Qassim, who also applied to come to Canada, was arriving tonight. For the first time in three long and lonely years, Imran would have the company of someone who knew him well. Someone who understood where he came from.

It was a cool misty evening, but he did not feel the chill as he walked from the bus stop to his little attic apartment. Imran could not wait to show Qassim his new home and city. The very evening that Qassim arrives, Imran suggests a trip downtown.

Sitting in the back of the streetcar
They stare wide-eyed at the
Electric and concrete jungle
Stretching before them
Filled with stoic skyscrapers
Lights shimmering in
The crisp
Fall air
Traffic light sentinels
Directing a symphony of movement
Hot smelly air
Being expelled
From sidewalk grates
Sights
Sounds
Smells
Enticing the senses

Although Imran has walked and travelled by these buildings a hundred times before, he is caught up in his friend's child-like wonder. With fresh eyes, he discovers his Toronto once again.

Hopping off the streetcar, they stop at a Tim Hortons for hot chocolate. Cradling the warm cups in their shivering hands, they begin to explore Yonge Street.

Streets bustle with life
Hearts beat
In synchronicity
Building lights
Against the backdrop of
The fuscous sky
Streetlights stand
Like lighthouses
Warm spotlight intermittently buffeted
By the receding twilight
Eyes filled with
Wonder and incredulity
Nostrils filled with
The savoury smell of hotdogs
Buzzing pedestrians making
Beelines to
Their hives
Car horns periodically
Punctuate the city's
Pulsing serenade

Part III – The Journey

The two friends sit in the Eaton Centre mall and watch people go by. Everyone is caught up in his or her own world. Each on a specific mission. Lovers holding hands, shoulders kissing as they whisper to each other, eyes greedily soaking each other in. Smartly dressed businessmen walking purposefully to some important meeting. Mothers unsuccessfully trying to keep their children in tow. At the lunch hour, Toronto is alive and bustling with activity.

Imran tells Qassim that he likes to sit and look at these people and imagine what their lives are like—surely more interesting than his. As they talk, he secretly promises himself to have a life like that one day.

In the fullness of time, Qassim got married and moved out. Imran, alone once again, decides that he wants a change. He wants to learn about the country he now calls home, to discover Canada. He decides to move to Calgary, Alberta and chooses to take the train so as to see the country.

The hum of the train and the rhythmic
Cha-chack, cha-chack of the wheels on
Steel rails
Interrupted by a mournful
Whistle
Piercing the night
The monotonous hum is reminiscent of
The Gardiner Expressway
I am overwhelmed
At the spectacle of
Canada
Mirrored lakes
Lush green forests
Quaint little villages
Stately bridges
Breathtaking mountains
Even the darkness is filled with
Transcendental beauty
The railway
Stealthily traverses the landscape
Serpentine
Meandering
Each kilometre a new discovery
Astounding beauty of

Pristine woodlands
Unspoiled and untouched
Calm murky lakes reflecting
Geographic grandeur like
Mirrors to a heavenly show
How does one not
Fall in love
With this land

Part IV – Reinvention

Imran noticed his reflection in the dark window glass of the viewing car. For a quick moment, he did not recognize himself. Was this the same "Dalit" who was threatened with death by the village priest if he ever tried to enter the temple? The same Dalit whose father and mother were brutally murdered as he hid under the oak tree that fateful night? The same young man who always felt the sting of guilt wondering why he survived, yet thankful he did?

For years, that guilt festered in his soul and ate away at him. Whenever something positive happened in his life, it was there to leach his joy away. It was Qassim who helped him to realize that he was doing the memory of his parents a disservice with this useless guilt.

In their death,
You were delivered
With a second chance
At life
The closed door of opportunity
Opened with their passing
Honour them, my friend
By enjoying the blessings
Granted to you

Through their sacrifice
Grant them the favour of
Seeing you succeed

Part V – Finding The Way

The man he saw in the reflection of the window was smartly
dressed and had an air of confidence about him. He credited
that to his favourite professor who helped him to become a
teaching assistant and encouraged his writing. That professor
had been a mentor and coach. He had helped him with his
English conversation and small talk. "*What a strange phrase,*" he
thought as he let the words play casually over his tongue. From
experience, he knew that words, no matter how small or
insignificant, had the potential and weight to impact a
person's life.

Standing on the edge of tomorrow
Contemplating today's decisions
Second-guessing
Speculating
Doubting and
Deliberating
Must I reinvent myself
So that I can fit in
Or make my life a medley of
Who I was then
And who
I am
Now
Can I keep the best parts of me
And the best of
My new country
To create a new man with
Old values and integrity

Will I lose what makes me ...
Me
Or will I be a better
Human being

As Imran sat contemplating his past and imagining the future of this journey, he felt someone's eyes on him—surreptitiously looking up, he caught the averted gaze of a young Black man sitting in a booth ahead of him.

Imran smiled, and the young man slowly returned a sheepish grin. Imran mouthed "*Hi!*" and casually waved his hand. The young man awkwardly raised his hand in response and looked away.

A wave of understanding flashed across Imran's face. He was like that when he first arrived. Unsure of the acceptable conventions, many times too afraid to respond. The young man's parents returned to the booth with hot drinks, and the family fell into a hushed conversation. Imran returned his attention to his laptop, the dull reflection of its light upon his face while his fingers tapped expertly on the keyboard.

A few hours passed. The family had long since left; three empty cups on the table were the only indication they were there at all. As he looked contemplatively at the cups, a thought crossed his mind.

Was the young man imagining what an interesting life this person across from him with the smart suit and tie and the laptop must have? Was he dreaming of having that kind of interesting life?

The train whistle pierced the thought out of his mind as he turned once again to his work.

ABOUT THE AUTHOR

Brian Sankarsingh

Previous contributor to an IWA anthology

Brian Sankarsingh is a Trinidadian-born Canadian immigrant with a passion for advocacy and a penchant for prose.

Arriving in Canada in the 1980s, Sankarsingh worked tirelessly to forge a life and career for himself.

Sankarsingh is the author of two books of poetry centered around the immigrant experience, racism, and the human condition. He is also a feature writer for the York Region Sun Tribune on topics such as racism and the immigrant experience.

Sankarsingh wants his readers to think about his poetry as social and political commentary.

Connect with Brian Sankarsingh:

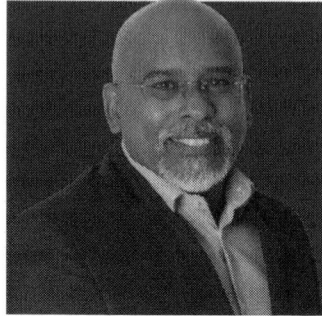

- Brianthepoet.com
- brian@brianthepoet.com

SIGNS IN MY PATH

BY YANNIS LOBAINA

I

When I was twelve years old, I read for the first time *The City of Columns* by the great Cuban writer Alejo Carpentier. I fell in love with the city of Havana and its magical streets.

Since then, I have always walked the streets of Havana with my eyes wide open. Mientras recorría cada rincón de mi ciudad, era como navegar en un gran navío del tiempo.[1]

If you walk like me, observing everything as if you were an archaeologist, my Havana will surprise you amid the unfortunate architectural decadence.

Mi Habana es una ciudad ecléctica. The streets of my Havana still preserve traces of stories from the colonial past. You will find hermosas puertas coloniales[2], some beautiful baroque columns, art déco and neoclassic style.

The streets are full of stories. Stories buried for centuries. Art in every corner and voices from the past everywhere.

. . .

II

For my fourteenth birthday, my dear friend María Anuncia Martinez Guayanés invited me to walk along del malecón habanero.[3]

In February, the breeze from the North Atlantic Ocean in the Bay of Havana is a blessing. The fresh tropical winter air enhances the true smell of the Caribbean sea. The sunsets are a dazzling spectacle that makes you forget your daily miseries.

We sat en el muro del malecón, in front of the Castillo de la Real Fuerza. From there we could see the Giraldilla, a statuette weather vane, a symbol of Havana. María, with a ceremonious voice, gave me the book *Stories of Cronopios and Famas* by Julio Cortázar. Before opening the gift, Maria told me I was a cronopio, and she smiled at me. I did not understand it at that time. Then I opened the present and sniffed at the book, as I always do with any new book.

Maria suggested I open it to a random page. And then I read it aloud. "The turtle and the cronopio" was the page that came out at the Azar.[4] This marked my life and reading forever. And like the cronopio in the story, every time I see a turtle, I want to draw a swallow on its shell.

Maria told me that, according to Cortázar, the cronopios, famas, and esperanzas are considered three types of people inhabiting Earth.

The cronopios are of romantic thought, of a poetic mind. They are passionate, with a tendency to dream, and with an ease of appreciating beauty.

Famas are like the antithesis of cronopios. Uptight, arrogant. They always have everything planned, they need order, and they are the most frequent among people holding important positions. And esperanzas: simple, indolent, ignorant, and boring.

Then Maria looked at me and said,

"From the first day I saw you, I knew you were a cronopio."

III

We stayed a while longer and sat en el Muro del malecón, observing how the sky was painted in brilliant colours of blue, reddish, orange, and yellow, reflecting on the waters of the sea. When the sun was almost lost on the horizon, we returned home.

As we walked through the alleys of my Havana on the way home, Maria advised me to read all kinds of literature. And then she encouraged me to learn other foreign languages. "To better understand the world," she used to say. We stopped at a corner of O'Reilly Street and Cuba Street to drink water. It was the only thing we had brought for our trip. Between sips, María told me that at another time she would have invited me to lunch at a restaurant. Everything closed, and el "período especial"[5] seemed to last longer than the government thought. Then she squeezed her eyes shut. "Don't lose hope, always read the signs of the universe and look at the sky, everything will pass." We both half-smiled.

I looked at the sky as she told me. My eyes discovered a shining detail in the building in front of me. It impressed me. I had been walking down this street for years and had never seen that shield.

I told Maria I wanted to take a closer look. It was a round shield, divided into three parts. In the upper segment, there was a three-masted sailing ship. In the middle a fish, and below a bunched sheaf against the bottom of an old plow.

The wide frame was a ring with the inscription "THE BANK OF NOVA SCOTIA INC 1832."

The building, despite the centuries, still preserves some majestic pillars. Neoclassical style, explained the historian of Havana, Eusebio Leal. With his usual enthusiastic voice, he told a group of Canadian students that this building was the first Bank of Nova Scotia in Cuba. "Famous Canadian architect John McIntosh Lyle designed the building. Lyle was passionate about architecture and strove to make every design unique and reflective of its environment."

Then, Eusebio Leal explained that the Bank of Canada, too, experienced growth in Cuba. Five branches in Havana and a branch in Camagüey, Cienfuegos, Manzanillo, and Santiago de Cuba in 1931.

"O'Reilly Street is named after Dublin-born Alejandro O'Reilly. One of the Wild Geese—the term used for Irish soldiers who served in foreign Catholic armies after the defeat of the Irish Jacobite soldiers in 1691."

The story that Eusebio Leal told the students fascinated Maria and me. He told the group that the next day he would continue telling other stories about O'Reilly Street, a street with many stories and cinematography-worthy views.

IV

Maria and I continued walking on O'Reilly Street towards our home. Hunger and fatigue could not overshadow the joy with which I reached my fourteenth birthday. María, more than my neighbour, had become my grandmother, my intellectual refuge, and my great friend. Despite the 50-year age difference between the two of us.

"The universe communicates with us through signals," Maria told me before saying goodbye in front of my house.

That night, I dreamed of the smell of the sea, the fish on the shield of the Canadian bank, and the boat. I dreamed of my eclectic Havana with large portals. Windows with colourful stained glass coloured red and indigo. The sky was such a deep blue you could almost dive into it.

V

In 2007, my friend Pavel gave me the book *Three Nights in Havana* by Robert Wright. It is about Prime Minister Pierre Elliott Trudeau's visit to Cuba. He had bought it in a Toronto second-hand bookstore.

Seven years later, I met my husband Chris. He is Canadian, and for love, here I am now. Once again, the universe showed me that everything is connected. And everything affects us all.

The day I arrived at the airport in Halifax, the news announced a very heavy blizzard throughout the province of Nova Scotia. This beautiful city on the Atlantic welcomed me at minus thirty degrees Celsius.

There was an enormous mountain of snow in our yard. The windowpanes were covered in snowflakes for an entire week. It reminded me of the Bank of Nova Scotia coat of arms in Havana.

A few days later, the sun came out. The sky turned a light indigo colour that made me recall the deep blue sky of my island. Outside, the seagulls and crows fluttered. I opened the windows and breathed in the balmy morning air.

That day, we went for a walk around the neighbourhood. At the end of the afternoon, we went to create my bank account.

When it was my turn, I thought of telling the person who attended to me the story of the traces that remain in my Havana from the presence of the Bank of Nova Scotia.

I couldn't tell him anything. The man was very serious. He kept asking me yes-or-no questions and asked me to fill in the lengthy form. When he asked me the address of my work, I replied that I arrived two weeks ago.

"I'm a writer," I told him. He didn't hear me, or he didn't want to hear what I was trying to explain.

Then he exclaimed without meeting my eyes, "So, homemaker."

Twice I told him no. It was pointless to explain to him that I was an immigrant. It was not his role to classify me as a "housewife".

While I signed more than twenty pages of documents, I told him I'm a writer. This time, my voice was firmer and more clear.

He answered me without raising his eyes, "Here, if you are an immigrant, you cannot afford to be an artist."

We were completely silent.

I thanked him and almost ran out of his office. I thought of Julio Cortázar's characters. I had come across a person with the characteristics of a "fama."

At that moment, I felt disconsolate, not because of his classification of me as a "homemaker" but because of his words. This was one of my cultural shocks in Canada.

I walked back home. I wondered about the attitude of this person from the bank. He was wrong. His frustration with and false stereotypes about newcomers made him say these discouraging words to me.

Only the pain of my full breasts sprouting milk and the piercing call of my little Amélie made me realize the passage of time.

So I wiped my tears. I breathed in the brisk wind and tried to forget the words of the man from the bank.

VI

A year later, destiny made us move to the city of Toronto. On my first walk through the town, I discovered a building with the sign of the Bank of Nova Scotia, now known as Scotiabank, at 44 King St. West. It made me remember the Bank of Nova Scotia coat of arms in the middle of old Havana. I smiled and repeated to myself, "The universe communicates with us through signs."

As I was touring the city of Toronto on the streetcar, I remembered my friend Maria. She always said, "We will find our way to our destination, although sometimes, the path seems to be a big labyrinth."

VII

Since then, I have been like the Statue of the Emigrant by the French sculptor Bruno Catalano. A great void appeared between my homeland and my new home. Being an immigrant creates a deep wound forever. The piece that we lack is an eternal hole never to be filled.

VIII

After eight years in these Canadian lands, I look back and feel proud of myself. Despite all the obstacles that others predicted for me since I got here, I have achieved some of my dreams.

My perseverance helped me not to lose my way or my faith. I was able to move on. I established myself as a professional artist. I succeeded with a few projects. And thanks to the support of my husband, I was able to stay home and raise our daughter through preschool age.

For my first four years, I was trying to juggle my life with endless hours as a new mom in a new country. And my artistic career was the fire that shaped my true character as a woman.

I had to fight against the opinions of people who still believe that motherhood is career suicide for immigrant women artists.

I have suffered from this harmful assumption here in Canada. Not only the man in the bank thinks this way, unfortunately; many people have the same opinion. This is a persistent bias in the art world.

IX

It was not an easy road; it was a great labyrinth with many complex decisions to consider. Finding the best way to feel faithful to our purposes in life is and always will be a path full of teachings. Good and bad decisions will make us grow, learn, and restart a new road in life.

Thanks to this labyrinthine path, I was able to heal my wounds and see how purple flowers grew between my past life cicatrices. Finding your way involves making tough decisions in life. Big storms, rain, and some flowers will always go with you. As my friend Maria advised me many years ago, "Don't lose hope, always read the signs in the universe and look at the sky, everything will pass."

---

1. As I toured every corner of my city, it was like sailing on a great time ship

2. beautiful colonial doors

3. on the boardwalk wall

4. random

5. the "special period" of economic decline

ABOUT THE AUTHOR

Yannis Lobaina

Yannis Lobaina is an award-winning Cuban artist, writer, producer, community art facilitator, emerging filmmaker, and photographer based in Toronto. She loves to explore themes of immigration, diaspora, language and motherhood through various storytelling tools.

Lobaina has published over 30 short fiction stories worldwide. She produced over 40 short fiction and documentaries in Cuba. As a photographer, she currently focuses on minimalist photographic storytelling, landscapes, patterns and pareidolias in nature.

Lobaina believes that art is an empowering tool for social change and peace-making. She developed bilingual (Spanish-English) creative writing art programs for children.

Connect with Yannis Lobaina:

- Enlareddeltiempo.com

ABOUT IMMIGRANT WRITERS ASSOCIATION (IWA)

Immigrant Writers Association (IWA)/ L'Association des écrivains immigrants (AEI) is a volunteer-run Canadian nonprofit corporation that provides programs, activities, and services that empower and support immigrant writers in their journeys.

Our mission: To encourage immigrants to express themselves more in writing, thereby bringing more awareness, compassion and peace to the world.

Thank you for reading *Finding The Way*, the fourth annual anthology published by IWA since it was founded in 2018.

Please leave a review for this book on Amazon.

The anthology contributors will appreciate your opinion. It will also help readers discover this book.

• Learn more and support our work: Immigrantwriters.com

• Get IWA news: ImmigrantWriters.com/upcoming

facebook.com/immigrantwriters

twitter.com/immwriters

instagram.com/immwriters

linkedin.com/company/immigrant-writers-association

amazon.com/author/immigrantwritersassociation

ALSO BY IMMIGRANT WRITERS ASSOCIATION (IWA)

The annual anthologies published by IWA are available on Amazon

Building Bridges (2019)

Grow Together (2020)

Moving Forward (2021)

Finding The Way (2022)

Manufactured by Amazon.ca
Bolton, ON